FOR THOSE WHO CAN'T

Thank you for so many forms of inspiration. You are a gentleman and true adventurer. I admire your scholarly pursuit.

Much Love & Respect

FOR THOSE WHO CAN'T

The Story of the First U.S. North-South
Bicycle Record

Brendan Walsh

Bicycle Brendan

Published by Bicycle Brendan
Bicycle Brendan books may be purchased in quantity. For more
information, please e-mail bicyclebrendan@gmail.com
bicyclebrendan.com

Cover photo by Michael Robinson- bds
All other photos courtesy the author

Illustrations by Harrison Howard

Book Design by Kory Kirby
SET IN ARNO PRO

ISBN 978-1-7366474-0-0

Printed on acid-free 100% postconsumer waste paper in
Minneapolis, Minnesota, by Bookmobile

Contents

This book is dedicated to my friends who we have lost due to mental illness and anyone suffering today.

Live in Love.

THE BLACKOUT CYCLE

T HE YEAR IS 2014 and I am in a constant cycle of going from binge to binge. It's my junior year of college and going to be my first summer in Allston, a playground for college kids getting wasted. In the spring of that year, I was drinking before, during, and after work, all the while seeing how many joints I could smoke in between the shotguns. Not a single day would go by without me getting wasted. It had been a slow build for more than three years and was obviously bubbling up into something. My work was a terrible place where we would crack beers at 10 a.m. to cure the hangovers from night before and many other poisons to keep the train rolling.

In early May, I bought a pocket rocket. A very small motor-cycle that had more torque than a semi-truck. Within a month, I had a terrible accident with the owner of the shop I had been working at. It all happened in slow motion. No turn signal, no time to stop, my front wheel clipping the back wheel of his bike... I was sent flying over the handlebars at 35 mph, skidding my face and shoulder across the asphalt. Miraculously, a friend was at the intersection who saw us take off at the light. They said I "looked like a rag doll skidding across ice." I was taken to my apartment to stash my bike where my roommates later found me bloodied in the kitchen.

After a day of excruciating pain, Olyvia, my now wife, came and took me to my parents, who immediately brought me to the emergency room. After some tests, I was rushed into emergency surgery. Turns out my appendix was on the brink of exploding inside me. I learned that you can get appendicitis from two ways, infection or impact. I had hit the ground so hard that it had swelled to the verge of bursting. My injuries included a torn rotator cuff and a major concussion. Most of my professors didn't believe my story and I failed a few classes that semester.

After spending time in rehab for my injuries, I watched a cycling documentary on the downfall of Lance Armstrong. This oddly inspired me, and I found my high school mountain bike. I began to ride further and further every time I saddled up on my Iron Horse. I rode that thing everywhere: class, work, errands. It filled a void that I didn't know was there.

A couple years later, I rode cross country for St. Jude's Children's hospital. To be honest, I still don't know what sparked the desire to head west. I had never even done an overnight trip before! After two months on the road, battling snow, wind, the boredom of local cops, and tornadoes, I made it to Seattle a changed man. Ever since, I have been constantly pushing my envelope.

I rode the "hardest hill climb in the world" over Mt. Washington that summer, completed my first marathon, taught myself to swim long distance, completed a half iron man and rode my first double century (200 mile bike ride) all in 2018. That is when I came up with the idea of the 10k project and how I could give back to the ultra-endurance community that had given me so much. The community that taught me to be resilient and to take challenges head-on in a meaningful way.

The "10k For NAMI" project was different from the "$4000 for St. Jude's Children's Hospital" cross country ride in 2017. When I rode from Boston to Seattle, 4,000 was the mileage I was expected to hit. It was a clear and concise way to show my goal that could've been perceived open ended. The 10k was going to be more that the cross-country ride. This would be pushing myself faster and harder than I had ever gone before. It would be more demanding not only physically, but mentally and spiritually. The stakes needed to be higher. $10,000 was a big number that showed I was playing with the high rollers and I was ready to risk it all for those in need. I also hoped that the added ante of a Guinness World Record would elevate the awareness for my cause. It was time to crack down and build off everything I had done in the past in a big way.

I hope that this book helps you in any sort of way. Whether it is to tackle a big adventure of your own or make a positive change in your life. Every day we make thousands of tiny decisions. Change is not always a big sweeping wave crashing on the shore of your life washing the bad away. It is the next decision, and the next decision, and then every single one after that. If life has a currency, it is our experiences. Constantly pursue the most moral and just action to better yourself and the lives of those around you.

THIS BOOK IS FOR THOSE WHO CAN'T.

THE ACCIDENT

ABOUT FOUR MONTHS before the 10k, I was training hard for my original June 17 leave date. I was putting in 400 miles on the bike and five hours a week in the gym. My mornings consisted of thirty miles on the bike followed by an eight-hour workday. I would run around fixing AV issues at my job all across Cambridge, MA. For my lunch break, I would either lift weights for an hour or ride hill repeats. Afterwards, I'd ride the thirty miles home. This happened Monday through Friday without fail. Saturdays were long ride days where I'd put down anywhere from 140-180 miles all around New England.

On one of these weekend rides, I had just gotten my second pair of cycling shoes and couldn't wait to see how they felt. I was feeling amazing on what seemed to be the making of another great 7 a.m. Walden loop. Coming down the west side of the last hill out of Waltham, I was cruising, doing about 25 mph when an Audi going about the same speed took a late left and hit me. Apparently, this driver really had to turn left. The collision hit me like brass knuckles. I was tossed over his windshield, somersaulting in the air before slamming onto the pavement.

Immediately, I knew it was over. The 10k was done, before it even started. I laid there in total shock, too afraid to move.

In that exact moment, a woman came running over and said to me, "Don't worry, I'm a nurse."

"Well, that's convenient!" It was all I could manage. I was taken on a stretcher to Newton Wellesley Emergency Room where all the scans started: head, chest, pelvis, knees and toes knees and toes. I had a concussion, whiplash, bruised ribs, bruised tail bone, torn meniscus, two massive bone bruises, and a sprained ankle. Yet no broken bones. When I walked out, all the nurse said to me was, "That was some superhuman shit, man." The only thing I could think was, *How's my bike?*

Later at the Weston Police station, I waited patiently to fill out a police report as they dealt with a multi-car accident that had resulted in a fire. I didn't mind the delay. That is, until I saw Gary Truman, my first road bike ever, mangled and squealing in an aluminum pretzel. My dreams were truly crushed. In the moment, I couldn't make sense of why it had happened, but understanding would have to come later. That evening, I sat in my living room with my parents drinking beer, overwhelmed by adrenaline.

I was injured during my senior year of track. I remember sitting, head in hands, as my coach said to me, "Sometimes bad things happen to good people." I hoped this was another one of those times.

The next month was a bit of a whirlwind. I was a groomsman in my buddy Dan's wedding, and a few days after the accident, Olyvia and I decided that we had been engaged long enough and wanted to get married ourselves. We threw together a little wedding with our family and best friends at the gazebo in Waltham Commons. I couldn't have imagined a better day.

Despite making progress, I was still trying to heal while dealing with life and work. Putting my dreams on hold was tough. I had terrible PTSD for weeks after the accident. I couldn't sleep at night, not only from the trauma of the accident, but also from the immense amount of energy I had built up and had no outlet for. I felt like a hermit crab out of my shell. Any loud noise or street crossing sent my head spinning. It was only until I really began my meditation practice when my demons settled down.

Meditation was there when everything became so unexpectedly quiet. I had first learned about the practice through Dan

Harris on the "Rich Roll" podcast. Even though I was learning more about the practice, there wasn't anything more to it. Not until I watched the documentary "Heal". The film goes deep into our psyche of trauma-related events. I watched it twice in one day after discovering it. This was the first time that I let my guard down, not to the world but to myself. Something needed to be done on the inside before my body could begin to heal itself.

It began with short, guided meditations using an app on my phone. The lessons began to build upon each other, just a few minutes at a time, whenever I needed it. Incrementally I was disarming my mind and central nervous system. My mind began to still, really for the first time since I was a kid, not just since the accident. For once, my mind wasn't like a beehive in the middle of a war zone. No negative self-talk, no cycle of anxious thoughts. Just brief glimpses of actual stillness. It felt like I had superpowers.

I was always the "fidgety skeptic", the one who ran, cycled, swam his way to inner peace. Eventually, I realized that I was only working on part of the puzzle. While I was getting huge benefit through intense training, I never really sat with myself. Though I made sure to train in solitude—almost every one of the 8,000 miles I had ridden were alone—I never just sat there.

I mean totally and completely sat. If you haven't tried it before, you are missing out on your full potential.

There was a huge outpouring of support after the accident. Gary Truman had been totaled, but tons of people donated to get me a new bike. With their help, I was able to replace the bike. Only a couple days after getting hit, as I scrolled through eBay at 2 in the morning, I found a carbon frame of the exact same GT Grade that I had planned to ride. I bought it on the spot and began piecing it together.

I went to physical therapy two to three times a week and slowly began riding again. Every day I would conquer another fear, traveling farther and farther. First, it was just around the block by my house. That led to leisurely strolls along the Charles River. Eventually, nearly two months after the accident, I rode a century on my Surly Disc Trucker, Sir Lee Richard Truckerson, my cross-country steed. Not long after, the second iteration of Gary Truman was born. Due to his jet-black colors and screaming loud rear hub he was given the name John Quick. It was time to get back to the grind. My fire was now burning hotter than ever. Now, not only did I have something to prove, people believed in me and I was going to do everything to prepare for battle.

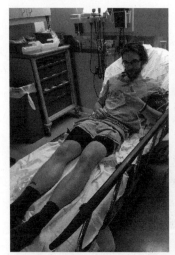

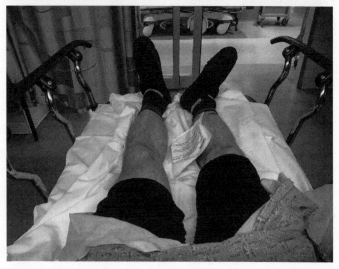

THE SHAKEDOWN

THE 10K WAS going to be my second "big bike adventure". The only other being the St. Jude's fundraiser where I had ridden my bike 4,000 miles over two months from my shitty Allston, Massachusetts apartment to Seattle, Washington. I had never been on any overnight trip before that, and this record-setting ride would pretty much be version 2.0. Working full time and dealing with the accident earlier this year, I only could do this one "big" weekend before taking off.

There was always the idea of riding from Boston, Massachusetts to Burlington, Vermont ever since Olyvia and I started camping in upstate Vermont back in 2015. I wanted to simulate as closely as possible the distances I would be riding everyday while adding as much vertical elevation gain as I could. The "weekend" would be broken down into three days, creating a large triangle across two major mountain ranges in New England. The first day would take me over 200 miles all the way to Burlington, hugging the Green Mountains. Day two would be even tougher, taking me across both the Green Mountains of Vermont and the unpredictable White Mountains of New Hampshire to my parents' house in Portland, Maine. The "Whites", as they are locally referred to, are home to Mt. Washington famously dubbed "home of the world's worst weather". The summit has the highest ever record wind speed of 231 mph! The final day would be an easy 140 miles down the beautiful New England coast from Portland back to my apartment in Waltham. It seemed like the perfect way to troubleshoot any potential problems during the 10k.

This trial run was a real equipment shakedown. I was carrying everything I thought I was going to bring. The 10k was going to be the first fast and ultralight trip I had attempted. The goal this weekend was to discover what was needed to traverse such a large amount of landscape by bike in a short amount of time. My cross-country trip was hilariously over packed with everything from a French press to an acoustic guitar. This time around, I only packed my jersey, two pairs of shorts, and my rain gear. Just like any big leap in your life, it was simultaneously terrifying and liberating.

The day started with neither of my two alarms going off. Since you can't make up for lost time, it was just a matter of arriving two hours later. I had plans to stop every 60-ish miles with a WarmShowers host in Burlington.

Riding 200 miles or more on your bike can feel like a pipe dream when you are at the start line. It is always best to break adventures into digestible chunks, in my mind quite literally. I like to look at it as "riding to lunch", except you eat lunch like three or four times each day. Adventures are like works of art to me, unexpected creative splatter through movement and experience. Even with a steady hand, a painting in reality will always differ from the painting in your mind.

After my first stop in my hometown of Ashburnham, Massachusetts, I was going into unknown territory. Despite having driven this route many times, as a kid, I had never traversed it by bicycle.

From the edge of town in Keene, New Hampshire, where I stopped for lunch, there was a palpable energy. It just so happened to be the "Keene Music Festival" and live music was coming from everywhere. One of those days where everyone is smiling and interested. Trying my best to multitask, I plugged in my phone and refilled my hydration pack. This was fairly chaotic for how often I had done this in reality. Fumbling and bouncing off the door frame, I went back and forth until my food was ready. After a burrito the size of a child, it was time to set off to the space between places.

Climbing the valley out of Keene, I knew it was going to be a big day. If you have ever driven through Vermont, you know how relentless the hills are. The pattern of up and down was hard work physically but helped me stay focused. With every heart bumping, undulating mountain pass was a glorious descent past farms and quaint Vermont villages.

By the time the sun was down, I was still in the mountains of New England and it got cold! Wearing my full rain gear, after getting lost in the woods and white knuckling 16% grade dirt down hills just outside of Burlington, I rolled into Denny's at 1 a.m. I destroyed several orders of hash browns drowned in ketchup for "calories and salt" Dirt covered and smiling I mangled my first late night "ultra" meal. A massive plate of an eggless veggie scramble (as I am a vegan) and several orders of hash browns drowned in ketchup. This salty, glycogen bomb was exactly what I needed to sustain this massive effort. It was only a half mile to my new friend Steve's house who would be hosting me that evening. It only a blink of an eye before passing out at a WarmShowers host that was left unlocked for me.

All of these problems happening during my mini three-day

adventure is the best prep I could've gotten for the trip. I granted myself five hours of sleep so I could be reasonably rested for the day. This day would be even harder than the day before. I would start by passing over the Green Mountains, a series of more than hour-long climbs to the peaks of ski slopes that are packed during the winter. Losing all the elevation I would work so hard for, I'd bomb down into the next valley. These would eventually lead up to the White Mountains, New England's biggest and baddest mountain range.

This range houses Mount Washington—"home of the world's worst weather", and the tallest mountain in the North East—and countless 4,000-ft mountains. A popular feat is to hike all those bad boys. (Something for a later date!) During the ride, I stopped to see my brother, Jamie, who lived in the town of Bethlehem as a mountain guide. He is a genuine Thoreau kind of gentleman. Built his own house with plumbing and solar power by himself, a true scholar who only completed the tenth grade. Our Thai food dinner was much needed, but we hung out for over an hour, something I would need to work on for the future. I almost made the call and stayed in his cabin right there but then thought of the repercussions. I would be cutting my goal short, even before starting the damn adventure. It was time to soldier on.

Soon after this, I began the massive climb of the Lincoln Gap, an intersection of all things adventure. Right before cresting the summit, I was gifted with some of that awful weather and had to put on my rain gear, the only extra clothes I had, as I went down the eastern face. I was picked out by some hikers and we all cheered together as they saw me pop over and tuck in for the descent. This was a no-joke, stomach-dropping, 13% grade where I could only see the fifteen feet in front of me. During times like this, all you can do is breathe and not grip the bars or get too squirrelly. Once I was down the backside, I realized everything was closed. Scanning Google Maps while steadily descending from the Whites, I found a 24-hr Dunkin' Donuts in Crawford Notch, the hub of the White Mountains. I was tempted once again by hotels and soft sheets, but a bagel and espresso seemed to fit this tale much better. At "Dunks", as we call them in New England, I chatted for a while with a woman of deep wisdom. I somberly told her how I was feeling: tired, sore, wah, wah, wah. All she said was, "You're out here doing what you love. You aren't chained to some desk; you are following your dreams."

Leaving Dunks was tough, there was nothing from here until Portland, sixty miles away. I rode through the pitch-black fall night, barely dodging wet train track crossings. This was also where I developed the "arm flap". When a monster 18-wheeler was approaching, going about 60 mph, I'd shake out my arms to contrast against the voided backdrop of the night. I credit this to getting me to my folks' place that morning. A 4:30-a.m. arrival near sunrise gave me the confidence that I could actually pull this out of my ass. I drank a beer in the shower while my dad drank black coffee, a common routine I would do in high school with my dad. I would be up through the night, go for a run and workout at around 4, and pretend I was just waking up so he wouldn't get mad. "People don't change; they grow," my father would always say.

I knew that the weeks ahead would be a challenge. I felt more prepared for what was to come, but, looking back, it was impossible to realize just how many challenges there would be.

THE DRIVE UP

I T TOOK ME over a year to even get here. The days leading up to this moment were an absolute blur. Taking time off from my job at the university, getting everything prepped, final adjustments on John Quick, mailing out food drops and t-shirts. I think there is more sense made in the aftermath of a hurricane.

After a great night of drinks and dinner celebrating my mother's birthday, we headed north the following morning. Like really REALLY North. The kind that people just respond with "Ok" and not the trendy "out there" where influencers take Instagram pictures. My wife borrowed her grandmother's SUV so she could drive up and follow me for the first two days. With a fully loaded Ford Edge and no idea what the hell we were both in for, we headed north in rush hour traffic out of Boston. We made the best of the drive by playing I-Spy and categories and listening to old music. There is no time wasted when I'm with that woman.

Many people have a physical support team. What I lacked in terms of physical support was made up in moral support. My wife is a fucking rockstar. Absent father, abusive alcoholic stepfather, and many other trials and tribulations warrant the telling of her own story. None of this would have even started without her.

There was an eerie calm in the gentle rain blanketing the great Maine wilderness. After five and a half hours of driving, we reached a clear-skied Madawaska, one of the four corners of the United States. Apparently, there is a motorcycle challenge to hit the four corners of the US in twenty-one days: Madawaska, Maine; Key West, Florida; San Ysidro, California; Blaine, Washington. And I was accidentally hitting two. Who knew?

We spent an extra day up there to "get prepared", even though we wouldn't have much of an idea about anything. But we made the best of it and tried to enjoy the couple blocks of Madawaska. Olyvia cooked an amazing dinner, like always, and I completed some final prep. I uploaded all my CDs onto my iTunes to listen to on the trip and made some planned stops for the next couple days. I wanted to just chill out; I knew I wouldn't get this opportunity for two weeks and had to take advantage.

Earlier in the day I said to Olyvia, "I wanna watch something lighthearted and funny. Happy Gilmore would be perfect to just veg to." After dinner I turned on the hotel TV, what was on? Happy Gilmore. That was the first sign I was doing something right.

MADAWASKA, ME TO BANGOR, ME

I WOKE UP AT 5 a.m. so I could get most of the sunlight. This was the plan I had set for myself each day. The clock only starts once I say it does. I double checked all my gear and packed up what I could the night before to make everything easy on Olyvia. She took a picture of me to post later that day. My face was fraught with both deep fear and excitement. I looked far more like a kid on the first day of school than a stoic adventurer.

I was already underprepared for the weather. Thankfully, I brought up a real lumberjack flannel to wear around town. There hadn't been any intention of wearing that during the ride, but I was so stoked to have it now when I really needed it. I stepped outside and immediately yelled to the empty streets, "Woah! it is fucking cold out!" I forgot what thirty-one degrees feels like, man. It had been a New England summer. I had "cold acclimated" to this before leaving, but I guess shorts and a t-shirt in fifty degrees on a bike really can't prepare you for sub-freezing temperatures on a bike for eighteen hours.

Before setting off, I started Facebook Live to document my attempt and share it with the world. My intention was to be positive in all my videos, no matter the day or the situation. Studies have shown that forcing a smile kind of shifts your brain toward positivity and actual bonafide enjoyment. Mine froze ear to ear as I started my first monologue. I rambled on about hard work and resilience more for my own sake than anything. Beginning to tell a couple stories, I already noticed my phone acting a bit wonky because of the cold. I said *bon voyage* to my Facebook compadres and set out.

I was only about thirty-five minutes in when my first bathroom break came. I crunched on some frosty grass to get behind an abandoned piece of yard machinery. The still quiet of this empty town, compiled with the frosted silence was indescribable. No one was around right now, especially cycling. The spider-webbed frost splintered across windshields and calming plumes of smoke billowed from chimneys of small one-story homes. As I looked around, I finally started to settle down and get a grip on the scenario. I was actually really fucking cold, not just uncomfortable here. Making it quick I got back on the road and called my wife.

"I'm so sorry, but could you please bring me some hand warmers? I really misjudged how cold this really is." The original plan was that she would take her time, pack up the car, and meet me at mile sixty, wherever that actually was. I felt awful calling for help fifteen miles in. I knew though, I had at least seventeen hours in the saddle, and frost bite was not a good way to start the day.

I made it to the Presque Isle general store before she was out of Madawaska and frantically searched for hand warmth. I entered the old shop, the floorboards creaking, and breathed in the sweet warmth radiating from its walls. Searching the dusty shelves, all I could find was a $2 pair of gardening gloves inside the Tim-the-Tool-man-Taylor shop. Small towns usually don't bring the biggest variety. Oh boy, did those work though! My gear was entirely slapped together like a patchwork quilt made of leftover materials; the kit was hilariously utilitarian. Everything from my long ass hair and lumberjack flannel to the ripped up running tights and EMS ski gloves patchwork. I laughed thinking about the ninety-degree weather only seven days away. That day was not today though. I swished and swooshed with my dozen layers to saddle back up on John Quick.

I saw Olyvia on the side of the road and she was trouble-shooting some issues of her own. She couldn't get the car WIFI to work, meaning she couldn't look up services or simply keep herself entertained while waiting for me. After a mere three minutes warming up inside the blue, steel-walled womb, she kicked me out and told me to hit the road.

It was peak "leaf peeping" season on the top of the world. The array of colorful fall foliage was like a Bob Ross painting. This is still part of New England, but it felt distant and foreign. I was born and raised here but still felt like an astronaut during the moon landing. On average, it's fifteen to twenty degrees colder early in the morning and late at night up here, so leaves turn far sooner than Boston. This, coupled with rolling hills, gave way to wild daydreams. Like one of those dreams where you wake up in a house that is supposed to be your own but it's all different and confusing.

During this stretch, I had to re-route up and around to Presque Isle where I planned to meet Olyvia. The construction worker holding the detour sign told me that "even cars are taking the long way". One thing I was really trying to avoid on this adventure was dirt roads. I know, it's part of the adventure, but my 28mm tires did nothing but slog through dirt, sand, or really anything looser than black top. I took his advice and his compliments, the first John Quick would receive, and took the literal and proverbial high road. It was rolling hills and tight corners all the way through the farmlands until it put me back on the road. This was difficult for me. I wanted speed right now, not scenery.

This was the first of very, very many changes to come. It was something Olyvia had been harping on me strongly about. I've always had a bit of a contradicting point of view on life. I am easy going but also want things to go my way, to go as planned. This was my first test of riding the waves. I wasn't going to let stress of things I can't control, control me. One of my personal goals of this ride was to work on myself, as we all should constantly be. I always want to push to become a better person and better partner to her.

After my first howls to the sky and the plateau of the farm-land, I met Olyvia in the parking lot of the local Walmart. To say we were disorganized would be an understatement. Someone blind-folded playing Edward Fortyhands could've done better. Bags of gear and food were everywhere, and I wasn't exactly helping either.

I rolled up to the car, laid my bike down, and stripped. This was me being overly cautious nearing the first nighttime shift. Staying dry in the cold is essential, not only to comfort, but also to safety. She had two peanut butter and jellies and an apple for me to destroy; perfect school kid and adventurer's lunch. I wasn't drinking as much as I should've been because of the cold, but it wasn't really affecting me. I stayed with Olyvia way too long. Leaving, I told her to take the extra clothes that she said I should keep, grumbling about overheating.

The temperature got into the fifties later, forcing me to peel off a layer. I had aero bars—handlebar extensions to aide in aerodynamics and to switch pressure points of your hand placement—that I periodically put those gloves on through. The constant transition was annoying, but, as the Boy Scouts' mantra says, always be prepared! This was almost a welcome distraction though.

After a while, Olyvia called, "You are going to love the top of this hill!" When I popped over the top, I was gifted a horizon Bob Ross would've stammered over. A symphony of fall colors as far as the eyes could see, complimented by tall, seemingly omniscient windmills on the hills' edges, peppering the horizon like steel-bladed giants. I had my first feeling of awe. It's amazing how we can be so simultaneously in and out of sync with what we need. This massive army of windmills looked like enough to power all of northern Maine, but no one who lives here will use it; the folks here are hardier than your average bear.

Not far after that stop though, I had to fly into a disc golf course port-a-potty. This was better than a trail angel with a bottle of water. I got in and shut the door behind me with haste. The space wasn't all mine though. Mr. Giant Fucking Spider lived there first. Being the gentleman that I am, I recognized and obliged. I mean this was his home, I was just lucky to share it with him. I have never liked anything with more than four legs, but I wasn't about to murder this thing because I didn't like him. Normally, I absolutely would've jetted. Since I didn't have much option though, I forced my fear to subside.

Along the way to our next location, I met more of my construction friends. It seemed like the whole state was getting new pavement. I could get little bursts of speed, but with all the construction, it wasn't sustainable. Our next meeting place was supposed to be a church in Haynesville. Olyvia went there first and got a vibe like something out of the movie Deliverance. She made us change plans. Moulton Borough would be the next stop instead.

At the next Walmart I found Olyvia, visibly irritated. I was hoping to have my stuff laid out, but there was nothing but snarls. This made me feel terrible. I knew it was going to be hard, but I didn't realize how it would affect her too. I tried to be quick, but it was another forty-minute, double-bathroom, snack-pack stop. This was something I would need to figure out. Though this was hard for her, I really couldn't take care of anything other than riding my bike right now.

My next shift was the most lonesome I have ever been. It was a dark sixty-mile, pine-walled, dog-chasing rut. I knew these times would come. Ones that would force me to comb through the dark, dusty parts of my brain that I shoved under broken picture frames. I just didn't expect it day one.

The reason I chose the National Alliance on Mental Illness was not only for my own struggles, but for the friends I have lost to mental illness. In 2011, my buddy Joseph Baker took his own life in the basement of his parents' house. This was ultra-complicated for me. To say that we had a falling out a couple months before would have been a bit of an understatement to me at the time. A kid in high school holds his friends in the highest regard. I'd felt that he had taken all that away from me for no particular reason at all. Not knowing why or what happened was the hardest part for me. Whatever he said to our friends was exactly how they'd thought. I was alone while everyone was out partying with the friends they garnered over the past thirteen years of school together. Even then, I never wished any harm on them or Joseph. I was hurt and needed my own time to heal.

I went to the funeral and put away my "Love for Joseph"

bracelet six months later. A week before this trip I put it back on. It was like two magnets pushing against each other when I tried to slip it on. My heart just couldn't make it happen, but my head made me.

I told my Guru, Hank "The Wizard" DeGroat, about the incident. "What did you expect?" he said, "You put away a huge dark moment of your life and continued on. Never processing any of the grief that got you up to where you are right now. It's time for you to put the work in to overcome this."

It was on that road where it all came back to me. I had been a first-semester freshman in college when it all went down. My life had already been a whirlwind of change. I had moved away from my small town. I had a locally successful hardcore band, High Hopes, break up and then lost all those friends too. It had left me with only my new dorm friends, whom I couldn't quite confide in yet. I had a crazy break up and started dating Olyvia. The flurry of phone calls from that night are like old tape recordings woven through my mind. On top of my human relationship issues, my cat of eighteen years who I had been with since I was a baby had died. It felt as if everything around me had come crashing down at once.

I remember trying to go to class one day. I walked slowly, step by step, up a back staircase trying to avoid everyone when I bumped into my professor. Up until this point, she hadn't been a fan of me, and I didn't blame her. I was arrogant and angry at the world. When she asked me what was wrong though, I lost it. I broke down to her and wept for the first time since I found out about Joseph's death. I spent the next couple days with my sister Sarah at her apartment a couple towns over from where my dorm was. Old friends reached out to me, but the damage had already been done, so I just tried to move on.

Now, on this desolate, dark road I realized I hadn't said his full name in at least six years. I looked down at the crimson red, silicone band on my wrist, tears streaming down my face, and screamed "Joseph Fucking Baker!!!" over and over. I can't recall a time where I had cried like that. I was hyperventilating, sobbing, and blowing snot rockets all alone in the great Maine wilderness. It was just me and him. All I could mutter in between broken breaths was "I'm so sorry, dude." Someone's decision to take their own life is exactly that, their own decision. It's hard not to blame yourself, but that choice was made long ago. The hardest part is the opportunities that he had, wealthy family, lots of friends, etc. None of that matters with mental illnesses though. The only thing that brings you out of the darkness is light. I was all alone now and the only one who could show me that was me.

Arguably the hardest sixty-five miles of my life came to an end in Pottsville, Maine. I saw Olyvia and crushed a 6-inch subway sandwich as she refilled my bottles and got me snacks. This was the first time I actually stopped only for the planned ten minutes and sent Olyvia to the hotel in Bangor.

It was about to be the first night shift of the trip. I've never had any issues riding at night, actually kind of liked it. Here though, I realized that every food stop also needed to be a bathroom stop, but this wasn't always possible. It was a frustrating battle against the clock, time slipping right through my heavily gloved fingers. I passed the local hospital to use their bathroom, only to have to stop five minutes later to adjust my layers. Then, back on the road, I once again had to pull over and put on my rain gear as the weather turned. I lost all the time I had saved with Olyvia, all due to my terrible time management. Something would need to be fixed far sooner rather than later.

Eventually, I was finally cranking along a little bit. To keep myself occupied, I called my buddy, Max. He was one of those friends I had lost when the band broke up, but we settled our differences and have since become best friends again. He works as a cop back home and, like any good recruit, is stuck on the night shift. I was on the phone with him, about thirty-five miles away from the hotel when I got a call from Olyvia who was trying to get into the hotel with all our bags at the same time. I could hear in her voice that she was scared but trying to stay strong for me. Nervous as ever in a new city, she had a homeless person approach her. I was on the phone with her as she began saying, "Please leave me alone, you can't have my phone!!!" All I could do was to tell her to scream and call the cops. Neither would help the situation, and, luckily, she slipped inside before it got any worse. That was the worst feeling I could ever imagine. I was completely helpless, listening to my wife plead for help. I felt like a less capable Liam Neeson in Taken. All I could do was listen to her shuddered cries and subsequent sobbing and pedal 13 mph for another three hours until I could see her.

When I finally arrived at 1 a.m., I found her shaken, watching the shitty room TV. This was, inarguably, the worst hotel I have ever been in. The tub was coming off the wall, the sink dripped water, and the toilet sounded like a Stomp concert when flushed. The bed was stained, with holes in the sheets, and the carpet was bunched up all over the place. I guess that's what an "antique" hotel gets you. She was pissed about everything and tried not to take it out on me. I divided my time between comforting her and trying to get myself ready for the next day. After a bleak shower and drying off with a towel that was probably once white but was now a yellowed, seemingly bullet-ridden version of itself,

I forced myself to pass out. Olyvia used my down jacket as a pillow and slept on top of the sheets that night. With everything that had already gone wrong in the day, I was just happy to have done 220 miles and have a warm bed.

BANGOR, ME TO BEVERLY, MA

B EFORE I LEFT, I asked my early bird father to call at 5:30 every morning to make sure I woke the fuck up. Well, that came and went. I texted my father that I was going to stay in another hour, but he still called. I woke up after only three hours of rest to forty-five and rain. These are inarguably the hardest conditions to ride in. Back in April, on my thirty-mile commute I had completely lost feeling in my hands. It had been about the same temperature and hailing too. Rides like this can be deceivingly dangerous due to their hovering temperatures. I didn't want that to happen on the second day. I had another 220 miles scheduled.

I jumped out of bed and started my morning routine. These parts of the day are serial time savers or wasters. I liked to pack everything at night so I could settle down and prepare for the following day. I would slam a vitamin drink, Athletic Greens, and eat whatever morning snacks I had, usually a banana and a BoBos bar. This dump of a hotel didn't offer breakfast, but I'm sure it would've been filled with moths anyways. After eating, I reluctantly helped Olyvia carry stuff out to the car and said goodbye, knowing I would see her in a couple hours.

An all-day effort is much different than going out to smash a century, then grilling food and sucking down some cold ones with your homies. The body's temperature is lower and, since I knew I'd be exposed for more than seventeen hours, I needed to stop things from getting cold before they started.

I overdressed big time. Right away my body didn't know how to handle the temperature and I had to stop. I took off a few layers and packed them away. You can always buy another piece of gear or make another dozen changes when planning a big adventure. One of these purchases was a full set of highlighter yellow Gore-Tex active rain gear. Today, I was unbelievably grateful for it. I was essentially living in this and it was paying dividends. Anyone who has elevated their heart rate in traditional rain gear knows why. The feeling of being kidnapped, wrapped up in a tarp, and brought somewhere to be buried alive. These things actually breathed and were hi-vis. At night, they were great for the arm flap technique that I developed back in the White Mountains.

The first half of the ride today would be equivalent to all the cumulative climbing I did yesterday. I rode in the rain for two and a half hours along the Maine countryside before the first stop at 93 in Unity. A quaint little coffee shop with a very kind owner set up in this liberal town in the middle of Trump country Maine. I slammed one of their coffees and ate a peanut butter bagel while Olyvia filled up my water and charged my Garmin. This was maybe the first good stop where I did everything in about twenty minutes. It's all a game of small victories through incremental progress. The perspective of riding more than 200 miles a day is daunting when you look at it all at once. Like during my practice ride, I kept telling myself that I was just riding to lunch, sixty or so miles at a time, three to four times a day.

I was back on the road, and the second shift was my first glimmer of optimism. I wasn't looking at the day's travel as another 190 miles but just as one pedal stroke in front of the other. When I would fall into bouts of anxiety, I would begin to count the pedal strokes on one foot. This is a common practice in meditation. Counting to four on your breath cycle—four in, hold four, and out four. Centering on something as essential as your breath really slows down the monkey mind. After the accident, meditation was the only thing that brought me back. For the first several days, I didn't actually heal at all. I was bound up with knots, both physically and mentally that I had needed to break apart. Through meditation, I was able to settle down again and start the multiple months of healing that I would need.

This section was my first change in scenery. It was still very rural Maine, but now I was getting closer to the lakes and ocean. Near the top of my first climb out of Unity, Olyvia called and said, "Just wait until you see what's ahead." I couldn't wait until I got there, thinking of the windmill farm from the day before. As I crested the hill, the massive rolling hills gave way to elevated farmland. I smelled it before I saw it. To my left was a twenty-acre commercial hemp farm. The sweet smell of this plant is only one of its endless gifts to us. Clothes, rope, oil, food, and medicinal products are just some of the things it can do. The dark green color radiated positivity to the sky and I hollered in excitement as I was gifted a long slow decent into the lakes.

Not long after this, I spotted another touring cyclist! I truly couldn't believe my eyes. She was fully loaded and clearly had been on the road for a while. We both waved and she said, "You're not the only one!" It was like she was reading my mind!

All I could think was how I hoped to meet other fellow travelers along the way, no matter the form of transport. Whether you are cycling, walking, or paddling, the experiences are all very similar. Being out in the elements regardless of their challenges or their personal pursuits is a unifying experience. There truly is unity in shared suffering.

After my brief encounter and a dozen miles to a pristine lake, I finally began to head south. With some sharp climbs I made it to the state's capitol, Augusta. It was actually a pretty nice town, complimented by beautiful homes and rivers. I liked the place. I went by a CBD store and was inspired from earlier. I needed to do some prehab before things went both geographically and metaphorically south too. My knees were already aching, and I needed to start the art of self-preservation. With a fresh jar of CBD salve, I knew it's natural healing powers was going to save me.

After another thirteen miles or so, I made it to the next pit stop to meet Olyvia. Banking huge turns and honking back at geese I rolled up to the parking lot of a Subway. O-Dawg was listening to a book on tape while she waited for me. I hopped in, plugged in my Garmin, and slugged half of an orange Body Armor. She also had a big bowl of quinoa and roasted veggies that I covered in nutritional yeast and eviscerated. I could feel its nutrients vibrating through my blood stream. Between shuttered, whole grain-filled breaths, we did some bike math, which told me something I was less than fond of. We figured out that I would most likely not even pass by our third food stop, our friends' house on the New Hampshire coast, until around 2 a.m.

My schedule had been more than optimistic when I drew it up. During training rides of 140 miles and up, I would always average a little over 15 mph. It doesn't seem like much, but over time it's huge. This is a game of small victories. A minute saved is a minute earned. But in conjunction with the weather and the hills, my speed was closer to 13 mph. So, by calculation... this wasn't going well so far.

The next shift was to Portland where my folks would be waiting for me. This would also be the true hilly portion of the day. Right away there were steep, loose dirt-road climbs. These are the times where keeping that positive mental attitude all day is essential. My predetermined GPS files turned out to be flawed. There were times when I would click on a road approximately .01 miles down and I'd be getting instructions to turn. My poor route planning was already biting me in the ass, and I was only a day and a half in.

When I got to Portland, I wasn't feeling too confident. Luckily, my parents and wife were waiting for me at Elevation Burger with a homemade sign and cheers. On the one hand, I loved it. On the other, I knew it was making me soft. All I could think was that I had to get going, but I also knew I wasn't going to see my parents again on this adventure, so I also didn't try too hard to take off.

My dad is one tough mother fucker, but he has always been very protective of me, especially as he gets older and my adventures get crazier. The reality of what I was doing was harder for my dad and Olyvia than me. He said, "You know, you could stay here. The door is always open, get a few hours of sleep and get back at it." Olyvia suggested that I stay with our friends in Hampton. None of these were viable options. I had a plan and a hotel waiting for me. I destroyed a super greasy veggie burger and fries, and then it was time to hit the road.

Almost the minute after I left, my sister called me. Her voice, fresh and enthusiastic, put a new spin on things. By her count, I could be in Beverly by midnight if I rode 15 mph and didn't stop. This was huge! It meant I could be done before 1 a.m. I started putting some power behind the pedals as the calories finally started to soak into my previously depleted bones. I felt fast and ready to put in work.

To make the b-line down to my hotel, I needed to change my route and get off the dirt bike trail that had been taking me south of Portland. Riding on that marshy, mud fest right now would nearly be like churning through peanut butter. This meant some difficult, on the fly logistical shuffling. I'd made this ride in the past, but whenever I had, it had been: A) daytime; and B) not so damn wet everywhere. These everyday, minor adjustments could turn a small inconvenience into a major problem.

To make up time, I jumped directly onto Route 1, a very busy main road. These are the times I am very grateful for all the commuting I do by bike. Freeways are always busy. Dodging cobblestoned streets and traffic out of Portland, I was eventually able to get onto the byway. The evening commuters' traffic was exhausting, but slowly it died down with nightfall. This section of Maine sees a lot of tourists. It's littered with fast food and ice cream shops along strip-mall-lined roads. Passing up on the scenic options was not something I would do normally, but here, I knew I was making the right choice.

I was making pretty decent time despite the dread at the likelihood of another late night. I made a very brief stop because, all of a sudden, I really needed a Gatorade. Usually, I skip all the processed high-fructose-corn-syrup nightmare fuel, but, oh boy, was I Glacier Freezin' right now. The semi-viscous, blue colored liquid hit my lips and sent me skyrocketing, even for just a second. It was also getting progressively warmer as I headed south and neared the coast, forcing me to shed all the rain gear for the first time. The sensation was conflicting. I gained a sense of freedom by removing this piece of comfort. As I pulled off my jacket, a slight gust wafted a rank scent to the edges of my nostrils. It had only been two days and I already smelled like roadkill.

Despite the time I was shaving off, the game of small victories was still not on my side. Cranking my way out of Ogunquit, I got a call from Olyvia telling me that my tracker had stopped working. I pulled over to the only streetlight for miles to change out the batteries. I had expected at least to get to New Hampshire before changing them. Opening the back of my tracker, I heard what sounded like sound effects from a Vietnam movie. Thundering propellers mixed with a constant buzz bombarded my head. I dove for cover as I saw a massive June bug coming at me. If you've never seen one, you might confuse it for a small bird. Making haste, I packed those AAAs in the back of the tracker, turned it on, and got the hell out of the trenches of June-bug warfare.

Not long after this harrowing experience, I began falling asleep on my bike and grabbed a cup of gas station coffee. Conveniently, this was the only twenty-four-hour gas station in Maine. It was like I was self-sabotaging. I knew forward progression was the real key to proper rest, but my decision-making seemed to think otherwise. With my GPS completely screwed from my route change, I knew stopping at my friends' place in Hampton Beach was too risky. Though there would be a fat burrito waiting for me, it would also be dark and warm. Like a newborn, I was already screaming and crying. I knew if I stopped there, I would be absorbed into the womb of their couch, so I pressed on. I called Conner and told him thanks, but I couldn't stop for anything at this point.

The New England coast through here barely touches New Hampshire. I felt a weightless sense of freedom on this familiar road under the midnight sky. This typically busy highway was my close friend. On a summer Saturday morning, this would all be bumper-to-bumper with people trying to pack into the beaches to eat shit pizza and yell at their kids. Now it was just me and one nice drunk. He pulled up next to me and yelled, "Hey! I love your lights!" I laughed and thanked him. At least I knew I could be seen here in the pitch-black night.

I knew these late-night finishes were going to happen, I just didn't expect so late and so early on in the adventure. 1 a.m. had come and gone, and I still wasn't in Beverly. In fact, by 2:30, I was just passing the quaint ocean town of Newburyport, Massachusetts. I knew I was the only thing on the road when

I passed a state cruiser housing a sleeping patrolman. I was weaving up slight inclines to save a little energy but also just to keep me physically aware. I was behind in the sleep game, running on only three and a half hours of sleep after riding 220 miles yesterday. Everything was looking like a bed, even the home and garden store, their bags of fertilizer like therapeutic mattresses. Over the last hour, I rode through a pristine state park with the wealthiest of inhabitants. Finally, at 3 a.m., when I came out the other side, I saw the Beverly Garden Suites. There I found a sleeping Olyvia on the couch with the TV on.

My late arrival didn't stop me from having to sort through what I wanted for the rest of the ride and what to send home with Olyvia. In a daze, I ate as much quinoa and roasted vegetables I could while slugging a kombucha. It wouldn't be for a couple days when I would realize the mistakes I made in that sleepless haze. I left her on the couch and passed out butt naked on top of the hotel sheets.

BEVERLY, MA TO DANBURY, CT

I WOKE UP TWO and a half hours later unable to sleep. Without any choice I began the routine of using the restroom multiple times to eliminate the immense amount of food I had to eat each day. My early rise did not lead to an early exit though. I felt bad leaving such a mess for Olyvia, so I stayed longer to help her and to pack the rest of my gear. The shuffle was chaotic and not very calculated. It was a stellar morning, so I couldn't imagine the weather deteriorating much more than I had already experienced. Out went my big rubber hazmat gloves and some other gear I wear in the most brutal cold rain.

When it was time to go, I completely lost it. I couldn't breathe and tears fell like rain. It felt like I wouldn't see her again. I held her in my arms like she was dangling off a cliff. She was being strong for me; I can see that in hindsight. She assured me that I was going to smash this thing and told me to get a move on. That there was still plenty of work to be done. She had to pack up our room at the hotel and then go to work. Olyvia is one resilient lady, and I needed her strength in this moment more than ever. I kissed her goodbye and saddled up with the rest of the morning traffic.

By all accounts, today should have been a lot easier. I had ridden at least half of this distance a dozen times before. I even made a last-minute reservation for a hotel in Danbury, Connecticut while lying awake in Madawaska before the start. My planned miles for the day would be 195. It was sunny and I was riding through where I live and work. Strangely enough, I felt lost at home. It was almost like I had never been here before. I kept getting lost and was laying into myself with negative self-criticisms. This was 7:30 commuter traffic in Salem, where everyone is pissed and cutting each other off before someone else can do it to them, a real dog eat dog kind of life. I still wonder why all these people are so angry.

Stuck on the pothole-ridden, line-hopping, two-lane highway that is Route 1, I had to jump the median to use the Taco Bell bathroom on the other side of the road. Not one of my proudest moments. My mistakes were compounded by early morning roadwork and rush-hour traffic. All of Everett, Medford, and Cambridge were under construction. I missed my bike path turn that I normally take to get to work and ended up in the middle of Lynn, a town so nice that is has a little tune for it. *Lynn, Lynn, the city of sin. You never come back the same way you went in!* There I was, standing on the edge of a ramp, with pissed off motorists ripping by at 70 mph, lost in my own city. All I knew was that I had to get to Route 16 in Watertown. I could follow that all the way to Connecticut.

Being a city commuter, I know the best way to get from home to work. I saw a fellow commuter who looked like he had refined his daily ride. I asked him where he was heading, made sure I was the legal drafting distance behind, and let him guide me through all the roadwork. I followed him until I recognized where I was and said goodbye. The funniest part was that he never asked me what I was doing or where I was going. If you're reading this, buddy, thanks for the lift!

After my *Tour De Commutour* I saw my favorite doughnut shop and made a pit stop. I ordered quickly, just wanted something comforting. When they asked what I was doing, they were shocked. One of the employees yelled, "You better get a move on, buddy!" I felt like a seven-year-old in little league listening to his coach. *YES SIR!* I stowed the delectable cold brew in one of my feed bags, ate the chocolate frosted, and tucked away the other donuts in my jersey pocket. I even passed my work on the way out of town. I was a stranger in my own home.

I headed to a local vegan restaurant at the edge of town to meet my buddy Jake, who had agreed to ride with me for the day. I pulled up and saw my fellow plant-based warrior. He was smiling, as always. We fist bumped and kept moving. Jake and I have only recently become close friends. We went to college together and stayed in the same dorms. Since our college was an art school, there were far more beers than pencils and more illegal substances than you could imagine. After college, Jake bought a house in Connecticut. We grew apart but stayed in contact through social media bike happenings. When I announced my record attempt, he backed it 100%. The dude even picked up groceries on a unicycle for me the night before!

He actually sparked my interest in big mile cycling. I started riding about four years ago, but he has been riding all kinds of cycling mediums since he was a kid. This dude can straight dangle on a bike. I saw some of his epic rides on Strava, having no idea people actually rode that far in a day. This day was the second time we had ever ridden together. The first was only shortly after I was able to ride again after being taken out by that Audi, and that was only a jaunt around the Charles with some Instagram influencers and their less-than-friendly hipster crowd. Never really understood why acting like you are better than someone is cool.

We rode right passed where I lived and all I could think about was going to say hi to my kitties. I knew I never would leave if I showed up, and Jake told me to stop thinking about it. With some welcome company and more dates than we both could eat, we stayed on Route 16 for hours. This was my type of cycling, direct state byways that you can just ride for sixty miles at time without thinking about directions. He's a fast cyclist but stayed close behind as we talked for hours.

We popped into a Subway, just around lunch, and I began my first attempts at a solo routine during stops. Charging my devices took up a lot of time. Not the actual act of waiting but getting everything out, plugging it in, and packing it away. The couple extra percentage points on the batteries were not worth the additional ten to fifteen minutes. Smashing footlongs and Gatorades, I felt more like a middle schooler out with his friend than some hardcore adventurer.

Before I knew it, we were at the Connecticut border. Right when we changed states, the hills began to beat me down. I could stretch while riding, but I still required a few stops dedicated to just that. My knees were taking a serious beating from the past two days of biking over 200 miles and more than 9,000 feet of elevation gain. I began to realize that today was not going to be anywhere close to a short day. Bombing city blocks with massive grades and sitting in traffic was eating at me, and Jake could tell. Luckily, this dude brought an entire pantry and kept passing me bits of food to distract me from the onslaught of hill-induced pain.

We hit our first arduous climb around mile ninety. This was the longest and steepest hill I've ever seen, even steeper than Mt. Washington. After I had ridden cross country for St. Jude's, I thought that would be a pinnacle of suffering. Today, this monstrosity made the Washington hill climb seem like a morning stroll. This was the kind of steep where if you turn around while riding you get vertigo and almost fall over from moving so slow. I'm talking standing and falling pedaling. More like scaling a rock face than climbing a hill on a bicycle. No perfect circles or 90 rpm; just knee-busting, tendon-popping hills. The kind where your car drops into first gear and the engine begs for mercy. In fact, hearing the cars' roaring engines as they passed us probably saved my exhausted, delirious ass from swerving in front of them while navigating these switchbacks.

As if my progress wasn't slow enough, it suddenly began to absolutely pour. The heavens opened above us, as if they wept for all human suffering. Cars slowed down to a crawl so their windshield wipers could catch up. Jake even asked me if I wanted to stop, since this wasn't in the forecast, I figured I'd brush it off. With no other option, we headed for the broad-leafed woods to put our rain gear on. There was no avoiding or hoping for the best, as sheets of rain came down through the Connecticut trees. It was a surreal moment of the reality of the situation, hunkered down to 200-year-old stone walls waiting for a break in the traffic. This brief pause let my mind settle for a moment leaving me vulnerable and emotionally needy.

Earlier in the day Jake asked me, "You've never done any-thing this big. What made you want to fly down the coast at breakneck speed?" I wasn't sure how to put it to him when he asked. Soaked and freezing, I started to confide in Jake. I told him about Joseph and all the friends I've lost to suicide and how I've struggled with it personally my whole life. Never feeling like I mattered with a family that was more fixated on getting their fair share rather than just getting enough. I tried to tell my truth while expressing the importance of my old friend's story of pain, one that is shared by many. He was very wealthy but always acted like he came from nothing. Noble but dishonest, I always thought. The judge can't also be the tormentor, so I cut those "friends" out of my life. Though I have forgiven most of them, some wounds are meant to be scars so you remember how you got here. Since it had been my senior year of high school, I'd still had plenty of drama to keep me occupied. For a while, I had new friends who all only liked my band. They would come to shows and we'd pull all-nighters, doing dumb shit because there was nothing else to do. After I went away to college, the band broke up, and those friends turned on me too. Not long into my first semester, I got a call from my boy Tim Belliveau telling me about Joseph.

The pain train kept on steaming ahead, now at full tilt. There were another few hours of climbing as we clawed up one rock face and bombed down the other. No one ever talks about the jagged peaks of this wannabe New England state. The rain paused, only long enough for us to descend one of the tarmac mountains to a quaint Connecticut village that seemed to have more breweries than people. This was the kind of town where I would fantasize about changing my name and never leaving, filled with smiling faces of people I'll never know. Unfortunately (or fortunately), my desire to raise money superseded my desire to disappear. We continued on.

I had never really hung out with Jake before this, other than those blackout, art school parties. The more we conversed, the more I realized how similar we were. A fellow vegan and philosopher, we bounced musings off each other for hours. After telling him the "why" behind this journey, he opened up, and I learned of his empathy. He told me of faltering relationships, which he had withheld a few hours earlier. The bonds of suffering are some of the deepest connections known to humankind. It's amazing, all the similarities humans have.

We stopped at a general store in the middle of the woods for snacks. Neither of us really needed any, but I could tell we needed a breather. "EARTH WORMS FOR SALE" read a large tin sign by the door. I stuck with the Cliff Bars. We were checking out and an old man was buying some of those dirt diggers. This gentle old soul started to tell Jake about his turtle while I paid. We had far too long a conversation about his shelled friend which only continued when Jake told him about the adventure I was on. He told us about his son racing BMX back in the day. These are the moments I missed about my cross-country ride west. I had grown a lot since then; now, I had a greater purpose.

We had several more hours of getting lost until we got to Hartford where I planned on grabbing food before continuing on. Jake was already late for his mom to pick him up and bring him down to the coast. Passing a subway, I knew this was probably the last substantial food I'd get for the evening. Burning down a busy three-lane road, we hopped some curbs to get into the metro strip mall. I walked in just as two dudes who had just gotten out of the gym across the street also entered. I looked at one and asked if I could cut in front of him, telling him what I was doing. Hesitant at first, the story propelled him to tell his friend. The cashier overheard my road dog tale too. He gave me safe passage and offered me good luck and fist bumps on my way out. People love supporting others with huge physical endeavors.

Jake and I began heading into Hartford just as night fell. From afar, all cities are filled with beauty and wonder. We made a quick stop so I could take my rain gear off and air out a little. It had been nearly three days of riding in rain gear and extra layers, and I smelled like it. Being a Connecticut native, Jake knew his way around. We went through the poorer portions of town, but no one had ill will towards us. Eventually, we pushed into the metro. Traffic was still heavy, and we were behind schedule. Part of me had no fucking idea how I was going to pull this off.

Just about a mile and a half out Hartford, I heard the sounds of cheering and clapping. I looked and noticed it was Michael Fucking Lashua! I grew up in a dumpy, rural, northern Massachusetts neighborhood with this guy. I've known him longer than almost anyone I still talk to. We ran track, used to train in the gym, and ran together at all hours. It was so good to see a familiar face at this point. I was feeling low. He asked, "Do you need any food?" I said no, but he immediately pulled out two sleeves of Oreos, which I hastily snatched with a smile. We took a picture and hugged before saying goodbyes.

When you are at your lowest, you come to find there are people all around to who want to lift you up. It's the Michael Lashuas of the world who shine the light on us all. A second before, I was caving in on my own misery. Feeling pathetic and not worthy to help anyone except my sad self. Now I remembered why I was doing this and sped off into the night. These are the reasons why we continue.

My saddle sores had become horrendous. The perfect storm: three days of rain pants created a environment for these wounds to fester; my shorts had no way to breathe. They multiplied as they bounced, chafed, and danced around in my salty, sweat-soaked shorts. On a bike path leaving town, I whined to Jake, pulling up ahead and mooning him with my pasty white ass covered in juicy, gushing, red saddle sores. I rode standing up next to him with my pants pulled down letting my wounded behind breathe in some early fall air. Jake and I rode for another couple hours before his mother picked him up at a CVS in a nowhere town. I was intimidated for my first true, solo night shift after this beatdown of a day. I still had at least sixty miles to go before Danbury, and it was starting to rain nearly frozen drops again. We said our goodbyes, and I went inside to get some Shea butter for my nasty saddle sores. The misty, night drizzle became rain again, and I was getting cold. I tried to cut the miles off by taking a residential street when I encountered a nearly vertical road, even steeper than its rural counterparts. I swear, mountain goats couldn't make it up this thing. Defeated, I turned around after uselessly murdering myself.

It just kept raining and getting colder. Foolishly, I had given Olyvia my big latex gloves. My buddy Mike called me, and I was distraught. I had slept maybe seven hours over three days and 600 miles. I couldn't even think at this point. I had to warm up and change my socks. I found an ATM and removed all my gear. I completely spread everything out and slowly changed. I sat there, feeling safe for the first time. Seconds turned into minutes and, all of a sudden, I had wasted half an hour in there. I needed some latex gloves or something to keep my hands dry in the nearly frozen late-night air. The cleaning lady was inside the bank and I thought nothing of banging on the glass to ask for some gloves. Mike put it to me plainly over the phone: "You probably look like a psychopath, bro. She is not going to let you into the bank." *Well, Mike, when you put it that way.*

He snapped into team-leader mode and put on The Eye of the Tiger. I've never needed that corny song as much as in that moment. I sang the whole song and went into the gas station next door. Scrambling in, I hardly noticed the bustling commotion by the register. I bought a watered down, gas station coffee and received the question that everyone does when they see me: "What are you doing?!" I told the cashier and gathering crowd the cliff notes version and watched their jaws drop in unison. "God Bless you, son," said a man who I would've expected to shake me down for loose change. I turned and asked the cashier if she had any rubber gloves. To my amazement, the cashier had food service gloves. Enthusiastically, she gave me two of those tacky, petroleum shields of warmth. I put on both pairs and felt like a knight, adding to my arsenal of armor. I left the gas station, ready for what I thought would be the final push of the night.

To my disbelief, after the gas station the hills only got sharper and wetter. I was going so slow that I couldn't generate enough juice for my Dynamo light, and my USB-battery bank had died long ago. It was drudgery. Slowly, I rode into Waterbury, a town I had been told "wasn't that nice." The streets were filled with what seemed like sheets of broken glass. Evidently from smashed windows by any of the people hanging out on street corners right now. There seemed to be more people out here at night than there would've been in the middle of a sunny weekend. The hills were relentless, stopping any chance at a speedy get away. A small child could've tripped, scraped their knee, cried, and still caught up to me. The coffee was also not helping my engine burn any hotter. Caffeine doesn't do much when you are truly exhausted, it kind of just gunks up the works and heightens your anxiety. I couldn't keep my eyes open. It was a constant battle just to keep my head up. Going so slowly on the bike was like being rocked to sleep. I kept bobbing, catching myself only to land into another bob. I was sleeping more than I was pedaling. I was on the phone with my wife going up the last hill in Waterbury when I said, "I need to take a nap." She gave me fifteen minutes, but I knew I had to nap until I woke up.

Just then, I looked to my left and saw a cancer hospital. I could see a warm bench inside. My muscles cried! I rolled into the parking lot and felt my heart sink when I realized they had been closed for over seven hours since it was already midnight. Because I had mentally agreed to my body's pathetic needs, I couldn't do anything but sleep. I leaned my bike against a bench outside, which I deliriously deemed "too small to sleep on", and chose the pavement instead. You don't always make the smartest decisions when you don't get a full eight hours. Under these conditions, it's hard to even commit to a decision, let alone make a thoughtful one. Without even taking a step, I laid down inches from my bike and dropped to the ground. Nervously pleading for my safety, Olyvia insisted I call her the second I woke up. With my clothes, shoes, and helmet on, I instantly fell asleep.

I woke up forty minutes later in an absolute panic. It was like a dream where you make a bad decision and then wake up to find you were dreaming. Except in my case, I was certainly not dreaming. The rain had stopped, but I was absolutely freezing. I shivered and my teeth chattered until I started to warm up. It was now 1:40 a.m. and I still had more than thirty miles until my hotel in Danbury. Now was not the time to question my decision but to stick with it.

These were the times you had to keep some wits about you. Luckily, my nap did help with that a little. Most of my lights had already died long ago, and I slogged through the rich suburbs of Connecticut immersed in darkness. The hills never stopped. I had to swerve to lighten the grades, passing through small town centers with cafes. When researching Dynamo bulbs, I learned about their watt-sapping energy. Though this one was only about five watts, my aching, lactic-acid-filled quads were too tired to keep it going, forcing me to turn it off on the ascents. Since I was going so painstakingly slow, it didn't matter anyways.

My saddle sores somehow didn't miraculously heal during my nap. Strange. To deal with them, I kept periodically pulling down my shorts through the streets of these sleeping cul-de-sac towns, even if just for a moment before the next cop or town drunk came around the bend. Anything to bring that sweet moment of relief.

Cresting the hill out of Newtown where the fateful Sandy Hook tragedy happened, I felt deep grief for their community. I tried to send love to everyone around me. Then, out of the pitch-black night, I felt a large mass moving towards me. This violent and evil shadow was moving with intent and direction. Fearing it was a black bear, I yelled, "YO!" into the night in an attempt to startle it before clicking on my high beam. A homeless man appeared from the shadows, as startled as I was. For some reason, *I* told *him* to be careful out here in the dark. His echoed response made me realize how ridiculous his side of the coin must have been there. Seeing a long-haired mad man, riding his black bike with no lights down a highway at 3 a.m. At this point, I was just happy the shadow was real and I wasn't falling into further sleep-deprived hallucinations.

It took me another hour to get the Maron Hotel. A beautiful, upscale establishment but somehow also the cheapest in town. This place had a fucking waterfall in the lobby for Christ's sake!

I limped on wet tile, careful not to embarrass myself in front of the overnight desk attendant who, honestly, couldn't have been less interested. I checked into my room for the remaining hours it was still rightfully and capitalistically mine. My wife had ordered a Domino's pizza to the hotel, and I devoured it cold, wincing and stumbling to my room. The first day and night alone had already broken me.

DANBURY, CT TO FLEMINGTON, NJ

I WOKE UP ONLY a couple hours later to the worst forecast imaginable—thirty-seven degrees and rainy. How could I possibly do this? Another 220 miles in the cold, wet rain? I was exhausted and the tendons in my knees felt like overcooked spaghetti.

Before I left for Maine I said to myself, "If it were to end anywhere, it would be just outside Connecticut." It was within striking distance of home and now beyond my experience in ultra-cycling. A total inconsolable wreck, I called Olyvia, muttering that I was so sorry, that I had failed. I put all this time and resources into the ride, and I hadn't even made it out of New England. In her wholehearted confidence said, "Don't worry if you need to stop, just start today." Her words began warming my frozen heart, sparking trembling hope inside me.

Immediately after hanging up with her I got another call. Knowing the battle I had last night, Mike called again after seeing my tracker stop only a couple hours before: "You haven't gone this far, to quit. You don't quit. You're Bicycle Fucking Brendan." Just like hearing The Eye of the Tiger last night, his words helped me dig deep into something instinctual that comes only when faced with fight or flight. I had to keep going.

In absolutely no rush this morning, I got my stuff together and went down to the continental breakfast. On my way out, the toilet's loose valve fittings began spewing water in every direction. I quickly shut the water valve, threw down the remaining towels and got the hell out of there. When I checked out, I saw a giant bowl of off-brand Jolly Ranchers and immediately thought of how I needed one of every color. The concierge passive aggressively told me to "help myself". In my primal state I decided to take the high road instead taking out all my emotions on this guy. I coyly said, "Don't mind if I do sir, don't mind if I do."

I left in a slow roll. I tried to be optimistic about staying dry, but it was a hopeless cause. My goal was to get to Perryville, Maryland, which was 220 miles away. With my adjusted bike algorithm now set to the "Rule of 12 mph"—one of many rules I came up with along the way, I'd divide the distance to my destination by an average speed of 12 mph to determine how long the day would take—I wouldn't get there for at least nineteen hours. I left at the ripe time of 9:30 a.m. It wasn't looking too good.

Right away I got on a bike path, gently protecting me from the near freezing rain, but it still was not quite enough. Within an hour I was soaked to my bone marrow, helplessly trying to manipulate a wet phone screen to find somewhere I could buy new clothes. I considered so many different options, none of which made any real sense. My latex gloves only helped so much, and my feet now needed a solution too.

I pulled into a CVS just off the path to buy some rubber gloves and get some trash bags for my feet. I posted up in the door to equip my Smartwool gloves, the two food service gloves, and my dishwashing gloves I had modified by biting off the fingertip on the right index and the webbing between the thumb because the large was too small. Getting four plastic bags from the cashier, I put two over my Smartwool socks and shoe covers on each foot. I felt less like a knight now and more like a body wrapped up in plastic to be tossed into the Charles river.

On the way out, a guy in a Yankees hat was walking in and made eye contact with me. Already agitated, I hated this guy for his stupid hat. (Go Sox, kehd!) As he went to walk in, he turned and said, "Nice day for a bike ride." Usually, my typical response to this comment is, "Every day is a great day to ride a bike!" But I didn't even bother; I was too busy fantasizing about choking this prick. Just as my sorry sap attitude was turning around, fucking Micky Mantle over here upended my hopes with his useless comment. The first real mistake I made was thinking I had something figured out. Reality was instantly checked.

I slogged my way to the Hudson River where I passed through old mill towns abandoned since the mid-twentieth century. More scenes from the picture book of my runaway life. Witness protection program would suit me quite well here.

I had to climb Bear Mountain today. This is a famous spot on the Appalachian Trail, and my excellent planning was set to go over the mountain. Due to the proximity of New York, there wasn't much of an option. Navigating that city would take up nearly an entire day; the chances of getting hit were much higher too. I had no idea what I was going to run into, but it was the only choice.

Immediately, I was tossed into a swirling rotatory which connected huge motorways on three sides. Car shot into roadway like pinballs. They had no regard for other steel-cased death traps, let alone a soaking wet cyclist going 12 mph. I had to have explosive bursts of speed to cross junctions while keeping my head on a swivel. Dodging chucks of truck tires, glass, and nails was just a part of the fun. The climb up the pass was winding and arduous. It was grueling, mostly due to the long, pinned corners and the heavy rain. I felt box trucks skin me and spray dirty water over me like waves on an unforgiving coastline. There was no way to be more wet than I already was, so I grit the sand between my teeth and dug in. Cresting the fourteenth switchback I saw the signs: Bear Mountain State Park. I looked over my right shoulder and saw a fleet of park rangers parked at a trail head. That's when I realized what I had gotten into. With the traffic so heavy and violent, I couldn't stop. With the danger of crashing or being run over it was way too dangerous. Bouncing around in the endless negative possibilities of my mind, there was no way out of this cycle of fear and doubt.

When I finally came to what I thought was the top, there was a fork in the road. I bombed down the top part of Route 202 and realized my GPS had me going in the opposite direction. Confused and defenseless, I decided to go back up and see where it had me going. Bending back up the mountain was both physically and mentally demoralizing. I had less than one bar of service on my phone to check maps, but I had no choice other than pause to straighten this out. Despite the circumstances

I'd made good time throughout the day, and this moment of waiting took only a couple minutes. But in that moment, I felt like I was holding up the weight of the world. If I buckled or faltered, it would all come crashing down.

My freshman year of high school I wrestled at the technical school down the road from my house. Though I didn't last the entire season, I learned skills that have stuck with me. I weighed 135 lbs. but quickly became the kid who everyone was a little afraid of. Not because I was mean or physically intimidating but because I wouldn't quit. I always ran a 5k when I got off the bus. I started in middle school for not much reason other than that I just wanted to. At the beginning of every wrestling practice, we would run for an hour straight up and down a slanted hallway. I never stopped. The seniors saw me fall forward, never doubting the finish and all joined behind me asking if "I ran cross country or some shit." To prove a point, the coach lined all of us sub-150 pounders up against the biggest kid on the team. When it was finally my turn, everyone grew quiet. I could hear their voices trembling with excitement like hyenas. They wanted me to fail. I dove in, wrapped up this 200-lb. senior and slammed him to the mat. The gym exploded with the pent-up testosterone of pubescent teenagers, especially the senior I slammed. This all culminated in the longest eight seconds of my life. Wrestling way above my pay grade (of 0) but also weight class, I was out-matched by this pimply, steroid troll looking kid. He almost had me pinned. I watched the clock go down in slow motion 8...7...6... Time had never moved so slowly. Even after that match, he never pinned me down. All I did was get stronger. Time can seem like it is frozen, but if you never let your fire burn out, you're the one who can control the outcome.

I stopped in the Park's mountain lodge nearby to dry out for a minute or thirty. I paused for a bit to admire the details in wood carvings. They were amazing. It was like the Sistine Chapel built in the mountains of New York. It was too early to stop and too expensive to eat, but I did decide to take advantage of their bathroom. I tried to dry off, but there were only paper towels. Removing my clothes and shoes I tried to get warm, ignoring the "Shoes and socks must be worn at all times" sign, which I assumed was intended for Appalachian Trail thru-hik-ers. I was on a bike. Totally different. I sat trying to dry out my phone and check where I was. Just then I realized this place was a hotel and that I needed to get out of here before I made some weak decision. As I left wet footprints through the place, I asked the guy at the front desk if there was anything to dry off. He disappeared to "ask his manager" and came back empty handed. I began gathering my belongings when he answered a phone that wasn't ringing, "Someone isn't wearing shoes in here?" I knew my brief bout of warmth was over.

Back on the cold wet road, I was tirelessly pushing on. Now descending the back side of this beast, I was getting filled with road grime. It encased everything. I was like the sopping wet version of Pigpen from The Peanuts. I knew I couldn't sustain this until 2 a.m. I began making some phone calls to some old friends. First, I called my boy, Max, out on the town with his new fiancé. I knew he would help get the wheels turning. Because I was about fifty miles ahead of record pace right now, I had some room to figure out a few details. I only needed to do 130 miles today. That helped me put the landscape to scale a little bit. Now, I needed to find out where I could stop tonight to stay on record pace. Services don't just exist wherever you want or need them. Rarely will there be a conveniently built restaurant/gas station/hotel hub of all necessities right beside the path. Realistically, it was almost always going to be a couple miles off route.

The road wound through mountains dense with thick pines on both sides. It was two lanes and had absolutely no shoulder, putting me at the mercy of every asshole of the Empire State. 18-wheelers, box trucks, and all their cousins kept crashing monsoon waves over me. I called Dan again, who was home at the time. "I'm legitimately getting concerned for my safety, Dan-O," I said. "I'm used to the traffic, but this cold rain is fucking with me all sorts of ways." He pulled up my tracker and path then found a town that would put me nearly exactly on pace. Flemington, New Jersey would be about seventy-five miles from my next stop. Off route, but it was my only option for the sparsely serviced metropolitan area.

It was now early afternoon in the Hudson River valley town of Suffern, New York. Aptly named for my current condition, because I was definitely sufferin'. When I had ridden cross-country, I had mailed myself a package filled with snacks and letters from Olyvia "care of general delivery". This is a common practice for thru-hikers while doing long hikes like the Appalachian or Pacific Coast Trails. I did the same thing this time along my route south, and Suffern happened to be one of the stops. When I got to the post office, I took my sopping wet shoe covers and gloves and placed them on an old, rusted 1950s radiator to dry. I was the only one in the place besides the two postal workers. I walked up, asking for a package for me and there were looks of disbelief and confusion from the woman at the front desk. Out of nowhere appeared her disgruntled manager. He must have been waiting to flex his little bit of power for years. He berated me, going on and on about how I "can't ever do this again" and how they "almost sent it back." Without argument I told him, "Don't worry, I won't."

With a new end goal for the night, I decided to make my last stop for the remainder of the day. The Dunkin' Donuts around the corner would serve me just fine. I bought a small black coffee and three orders of hash browns. I set up at a table and began the process of drying stuff out and changing my base layers in the bathroom. Any good bike bum knows that those high-powered Xlerator hand dryers are a godsend. Riding cross-country, these things have saved my feet many times over, though not the next occupant's nose. Changing socks and drying out my gloves breathed some much-needed hope and warmth into me. This was the first figurative bit of light I had gotten all day. I had an early night planned where I could catch up on planning and eat as much food as possible. It was time for me to keep moving forward so I wouldn't jeopardize my opportunity to catch up on sleep and calories. I tried my best to be efficient but also need this recharge before the last six-hour push.

Right outside of Suffern, Olyvia called me and told me that my mom had landed me a radio interview with a local Portland station WPOR. This was the first instance I noticed that my emotions were going haywire from lack of sleep and cold, wet weather. What ensued was some serious DC-villain, Joker-like erratic behavior. Out of nowhere, I started bawling my eyes out, then a sharp corner and laughter rumbled and erupted like lava from my cold and cracked soul. I couldn't have been happier. This was a huge opportunity to spread my message and to get more donations for NAMI. My mom landed this just by sending out an Instagram message to the morning talk show host, John Shannon. He loved the story, and a couple days from this dark and dreary day, I'd have my chance to go on the air.

As I went further through the sopping, slogging day, I started to realize the ripple effect of my "short day". Before I had started the ride, I booked all my hotels and mailed those care packages to said hotels all the way down the coast. If I were to stay on point, it meant my following day would be 300 miles. I knew I had to think fast.

The logistics alone put people off when planning great adventures. The 10k is a spiritual journey driven by the feats of physical and mental strength. You can't ever plan for everything. You will be wrong. Shit will fall apart, straight through your fingers and blow up in your face. But in these moments, you can't give up. You fight to adjust the sails when the wind changes direction because you have an unwavering determination to reach the goal. Not a chance would I be driven to a soft sunset, as a great story will never be held within a vacuum. It was my duty to endure and conquer the challenges for the good of those I hoped to help. In a world of instant gratification, this is something that is often neglected.

I called Olyvia knowing I needed some serious help. What happened next is the kind of scene at the end of every sports movie of the early 2000s, but with less slow motion and catchy hip-hop hooks. In a four-way call with Olyvia, Mike, and my buddy Matt—whom I aptly named "The 10k Crew"—we started to salvage the shell of the 10k. They were all integral to the life of this ride. They witnessed the birth and helped nurture it to the start line. Helping with media, training, and morale, they committed a lot of their own time to its success.

The following scene could only go by one name, "The Conference Call". Matt, Mike, Olyvia and I began planning. I told them how I had begun to realize how long I can ride in between stops and that days of 220 miles or greater made me finish way too late to have enough sleep or an early enough start. They found my tracker path and began chunking the mileage in between hotels to have days between 200 and 210 miles. They even found great vegan spots for the next couple days for me.

With a fresh outlook on essentially an entirely new ride, the forty-degree, rainy weather bothered me much less knowing I only had three more hours in it. The rain still poured fat drops like buckets from trap doors over me. The sharp glare and cold, sandy water blurred my glasses. I started seeing signs for high-traffic deer areas, which also did not help my headspace. Imaginary deer kept jutting out into my all-too-fuzzy path. Just before veering to the side, I'd catch myself in time to keep my wheel straight. I made one last stop for water at a sweet little joint, Nick's Pizza, right in the middle of Nowhere, New Jersey. This was totally a place where everyone is called "guy". Quickly doing my business, I came squishing back out to my bike. As I left a woman said, "Someone's bike is talking!" I had left the phone call going on speakerphone when I went in. I laughed and told her I was on a very important business call. No one is alone, even if you're the only one who can pedal your bike.

This entire moment was so powerful. Even though I was out here all alone in the freezing rain, I felt so loved. My wife and two best friends were helping clean up a huge mess. The owner of the pizza shop felt like an old friend when I asked for water. Even this random woman had good intentions with her hilarious DreamWorks movie world with my talking bike. It was a great reminder to stay strong during rest of the suffering I still had in store.

The rest of the ride could be best described as sad hope. I kept shifting in the saddle to avoid my aching, oozing saddle sores. My hands were sore from my anxiety at being passed by cars and from gripping the bars to stay upright over Bear Mountain. My poor knees cried out from the 750 miles I had done over three and a half days in the constant cold, wet weather. I looked like a drowned rat in neon clothing. The night was dark and all consuming. Reflections off the wet road even made it hard to take in the beauty of the scenery.

Everyone always talks shit about New Jersey, but even in the dark this place was gorgeous. The one major town I passed through looked like a Norman Rockwell painting. Houses had huge columns out front and rolling pasture-sized yards. Trains whistled in the distance in the dark night. It all felt very familiar to my training grounds in Lincoln, Massachusetts where the famous *Walden* was written by Henry David Thoreau.

The last stretch of road was a treacherous three-lane highway, but it was the only way to get to my hotel. These are hella convenient though, and the Applebee's next to my hotel made the risk worthwhile. After nearly passing out eating fries at the bar, I rolled carefully through several rear parking lots to the most motor-inn looking place you ever saw. Rows and rows of one-night, straight to the door off the highway kind of convenience. Waiting for me was a large Domino's pizza. I was about to destroy the daily recommended calories of several large men in one sitting. Words could not describe how happy I was.

There was still a lot of work to be done. I had to empty all my bags and turn my bike upside down to drain my waterproof bags. You know something is waterproof when you have to pour it out. Much needed drivetrain maintenance left grease chunks and dirt everywhere like a mid-west tornado. This was the first time I had time and a washer/dryer. All clothes went in, and I hopped out of the motel laundromat in nothing but my rain pants. I needed the short day so I could take care of everything. After this reset, I was ready to attack the next day.

FLEMINGTON, NJ TO HYATTSVILLE, MD

I WOKE UP AFTER five hours of sleep and still had to dry my shoes. One thing I do not like is having wet shoes the day after I've spent soaked. It was astonishing how much shit was everywhere in the room. The short day was intended for me to get some extra rest. The truth was all the extra time was filled with chores. Even though I didn't get an astonishing amount of sleep, I was feeling far better. Since I had to re-pack everything due to the rotting granola in my feed bags (and that was *not* cool), there was more work to be done before I even took off for the day.

Leading up to the departure date both before the accident and then again in September, nothing else but this ride crossed my mind. It was like an iron clad, impenetrable fortress that no shit was going to put a dent in. Focus like a Navy Seal ready to storm a compound. That is a characteristic that sets you up for success no matter the medium. I had to close a lot of doors to people who didn't understand where I was coming from. A lot of "Friday Friends" were mad at me for not boozing like I used to and were truthfully really hurtful and kind of backstabbing. The thing with setting your sights on such a huge thing is that you always have work to put in. It's not glamourous and it's not sexy. It just *is*. Look at the focus of Buddhist monks, absolute paragons of discipline. You find success through constant practice of putting in the work when you dread it like a bullet in the head. I probably should've reminded myself of this a couple times this morning.

After what felt like the re-organization of my entire life, I left with only a Bobo toaster pastry and a fruit bar for fuel. The road from last night was a very different beast during morning rush hours. I was just starting to realize how busy it was. Last night's downpour and no visibility led me to believe this was a busy road, but nothing like this. Morning traffic was just starting up and all the business-casual folk were steaming that some stupid cyclist existed on the same rock as them. The road I was on was a bonafide highway that allowed cyclists on it. In the western U.S., places like Montana, that's nothing special.

Here in the Mid-Atlantic these angry, buzzing worker bees thought I was far too close to their hive. Honks, shouts, and death threats were a part of my daily experience. A little early if you ask me though.

My re-route left me in a shitty situation with the Pennsylvania highway and bridges. A lot of them wouldn't allow cyclists, or they had some weird rule about going up on the path alongside it. After spending so much time being lost in areas where I have no cultural reference, I no longer get mad at tourists back in Boston. After multiple arguments with police, I was on a hobunk, no-shoulder secondary highway that felt like a tightrope walk. My one saving grace was finally having sun today. Vitamin-D, baby!

The vibes only kept me reeling for so long as I became utterly and completely lost again. Trying to comply with Guinness's often arbitrary rules of what roads we're allowed to use and getting held up by local authorities was wasting a lot of time. After inspecting Google Maps, there was a clear major artery out of this rundown town. Unfortunately for my adventure mascot Mr. Crabman and me, it was the interstate, where I was not allowed to ride. On the other hand, my Garmin was trying to re-route to a bike trail just outside city limits, but it was nearly impossible to find it from my vantage point. I ended up riding down some back alleys, which, oddly, were dirt paths, and cutting through a bunch of industrial parking lots. After an hour of wasting time and meandering, I was on the Chester Valley Trail shooting for my first food stop of the day at the Liquid Eatery in West Chester. This stop was a part of the whole itinerary overhaul with the 10k Crew the night before. I was starting to figure out a science to the quick food pickup. When I called and asked, "What has the most calories?" they probably weren't expecting me to please and thank-you. This is a game of getting as many calories as you can in the most mobile way possible. Milkshakes in my handlebar bags? Yup. A big cheesy, avocado panini for my jersey pocket? Don't mind if I do! Part engineering and part art, this was a fun challenge to momentarily distract myself from the task at hand.

The Trail ended up going over a monster hill on the backside of an industrial park and then bombed through an entire metro area. Before I knew it, I was in West Chester, home of the old MTV show, Viva La Bam. This was a seriously gorgeous city though, another "disappear and never go back to your regular life" kind of town. It was like being on the set of Sweet Home Alabama, where everyone is smiling and it's easy to find parking. The store front of the restaurant even came complete with "awkward couple on first date". I asked them to watch my bike.

They replied "Sure!" only to disappear as soon as I was inside. The walls were pure white and filled with hope. I can't even begin to describe the immense relief that my vanilla milk shake gave to my poor and oh-so-sorry tongue. I hadn't realized that I'd been crunching things down with my teeth and my tongue to eat faster. My nearly tasteless buds were sore, and this was like ice to a burn wound.

Without any rain, I was finally able to stow my rain gear and strip down to my jersey. This meant I also had to put on sunscreen for the first time as I was leaving town. Typically, I hate having anything on my skin, but this was another sense of relief. I passed the town's university and witnessed all the students buzzing around. Long boards, giant headphones, and backpacks zigzagging around the quad. One can only imagine all the places these young minds will journey. Leaving town was hard but becoming more routine again. I had to move on and stay focused on the mission.

A week before I left, as I was doing final preparations, I got an email from a woman named Lynn Salvo. Lynn is a two-time record holder for oldest woman to cycle Canada and the U.S. She let me know about a particular bridge I was going to cross on this journey in a Maryland town called Havre de Grace. I looked into it before the trip and called the local authorities for assistance. They let me know they would escort me across this bridge that had limited bicycle traffic. It was cars only except on the weekend, but the record gave me no choice but to cross on a Friday.

With my short day yesterday, I was figuring to be about twelve hours behind my original schedule, which would put me at the bridge around 6 p.m. instead of 6 a.m. A huge detour reminded me that I should call and follow up with the police. Completely un-aware and un-apologetic to my previous plans or agreement, I received a flat "No." The gentleman in charge was less than enthused that I even wasted his time asking. I pleaded with him, trying to use my record and NAMI to help my case. He tried to push the buck off onto every other bridge in the area. He coyly offered me the interstate as Option B. He even gave me the number to call the state police. Because of the detour, I was already going to miss picking up my supplies at a hotel and would add more than fifteen miles to an already long day which was just getting longer. To toss even more gas on the fire, I had to re-route twice just to avoid the godforsaken bridge that apparently even Moses couldn't cross.

The story here has no happy ending. I kept pulling over to speak to other people who were put on the phone, literally begging them to no avail. It got to the point where I was so pissed,

I was going to do it anyways. A not so well thought out "I dare you to catch me" move. In phone-a-friend fashion, I called Max to ask what would happen if I crossed the bridge. He basically told me that I would be arrested if I crossed anyways. I told him I was going to peel off my saddle sores and mail them to the station in Havre de Grace, but really this was the moment I just had to adopt the mantra "1, 2, 3. Over it." I couldn't do anything about the situation, so it was time to adjust the one thing I could, my attitude.

Backtracking north into Delaware, my new route sent me straight through the high farmlands of Pennsylvania. Enormous climbs began to smash into me, blindsiding my knees and hands. The assault began with some seriously steep ascents to a beautiful plateau of lush greenery as far as the eye could see. I gained elevation so fast it actually got colder. I started to do some bike math when I realized it would be smart to grab some water before I tried to push through Baltimore. Just at this moment I saw a man unfurl an open sign to a cidery directly in front of me. It was only this guy and another woman inside their quaint little farm house. In an attempt to be nice, I told them how great their place was and that they should use it as a wedding venue. I'm guessing my appearance probably didn't suggest I was an "inside cat" who goes to nice weddings.

Filled up to the brim with water, it was time to make my way to my next big city, Baltimore. Right when I was about to get on the main road that led to the new bridge that I had to take (Option C, if you're wondering), I got a phone call. A familiar voice rang through the line. "Good news!" It was the Havre de Grace bridge police. "We're going to help you get across our bridge!" This is one of those philosophical moments where you choose the path that you want to stay on. Instead of saying, "What the fuck! I had to change everything because of this, you useless waste of tax dollars!" I said, "Ah, thanks so much, but I'm already fifteen miles north, taking the other bridge you told me to. I really appreciate it." This left her astonished. "How did you get here so fast?!" she said. It made me realize that I had made the right decision and boosted my deflated confidence. It does feel good to take the high road. It did *not* feel good to go this new way though. The new route brought me over the Conowingo Dam which the officer assured me was beautiful and that I would love it.

I did not love it. Organ snatching grades made me stand for long sections of the climb, which made my heart pound. Not only did it put me into what endurance athletes refer to as "the red", but it also put much more pressure on my hands. The sensation was so strange. It felt like they have been smashed with a mallet a couple days prior, and now there was just this dull ache. With no way to actually tell when, I had lost my gloves a few days before. Pretty typical thing for me, but now I'd have to pay for my careless mistake. The worst part was that I had begun to lose feeling in my hands. I would learn later that the nerves in both hands had become compressed in one area and pinched in another. All this extra pressure just meant it would only continue to get worse. The stress impaired the motor skills along the anatomical inside of my hands and really weakened their overall strength. It was getting to the point that I had to shift with my opposite hands because they weren't strong enough. I knew nothing about it at the time. I simply laughed it off and continued mashing them into the hoods of my handlebars.

I couldn't believe these unrelenting hills. It went on for hours and hours. Why the hell did no one ever say Maryland was so damn hilly? My speed was utterly dismal. I was just fighting to stay up at times and not completely burn out. The evening sun was a deep, tropical orange and purple as it faded to black behind the rich metro of Baltimore while I battled its unrelenting hills.

Nightfall soon set in and I was still frustrated with my speed. With less than a thought, I pulled over in someone's driveway to quickly take care of business. Around this point of near desperation, all inhibition goes out the window. I was hard pressed to even lift a leg over the crossbar let alone scamper off into the protected woods that seems to be everywhere except where I had stopped. The top of this long gravel driveway would have to do. On cross-country trips like this, there isn't always easy access to bathrooms or even a suitable substitute, so I developed a trick to avoid suspicion. With the bike wedged between me and the Earth, I'd lean against it and just let it rip. So laid back and cool like that, no one would think twice. But seriously, what are the chances that the owners would come home just then? With traffic seeming to lead outside the city right now, evidently chances were pretty good. I'd been through enough shit with the police already today, so I hastily took off into the cold night.

It was now just after 8 p.m. After a huge winding descent, passing more and more run-down buildings, I was just getting to the outskirts of Baltimore. Being in a city again, there were chores to do. I had missed a food drop due to my helpful police interactions, so I knew I needed some dinner and snacks for the future. Baltimore is laid out the same as every city I've ever ridden through. The outer edge is beautiful. Everyone there must be an award-winning, New York Times best-selling author. Then, as boring as any cookie-cutter housing development across America, the nice suburbs run into some strip malls.

Despite how they can all blend together, I love coming into new cities. I always cherish my time in them because I love people and I love to hear their stories. Being in a new big city is always exciting at first, and Baltimore was no different. Looking around seeing how people operate, watching the organism move and breathe. Being from Boston, I felt no surprise seeing cars literally parked in the road with their hazard lights on. I was in full on commuter mode, dodging people, swerving lanes.

In my normal day-to-day, I would never eat at Chipotle. This wasn't how I usually operated though. I ripped left into a parking lot, leaned my bike against the huge window and went inside. After I paid, I ran back outside to my bike to get to my next task. With a fat, warm burrito slapped together and stuffed in my pocket, dinner was set. Now time for the road fuel. Right across the street was stop two: 7-Eleven. They have the supreme bike fuel, Lenny and Larry's cookies. These monster vegan cookies are practically a whole meal. They're over 400 calories and really do fill you up. There was no wasting time. I brought in my own bag, filled it, and waddled to the counter. As I gave my change to the guy behind me (it can really weigh you down), the cashier asked me what I was doing in Baltimore. I gave him the spiel and told him how far I'd already gone up to this point. His smile was genuine and contagious, and I left feeling proud with my bag of snacks. Back on the road, dressed in neon clothing on a loud carbon bike with seven lights, I was a beacon moving through the city.

Since my detour had forced me into the city a different way than I had planned, my Garmin was more useless than keeping all that change. I was using Google Maps to direct me through the city. I started to see "road closed" signs. Google kept telling me "straight ahead" as I bombed down the hill. It led to another detour, but on a bike, that means nothing... unless it's a bridge. Clearly, nobody uses Google Maps around here. Cutting around signs that were practically rotting, I found myself in a park that had clearly closed years ago. At an abrupt halt I looked around at construction completely abandoned with a huge mound of earth. Noise rushed out from beside me. I whipped my head around as, to my amazement, deer began leaping through the tall grass that sprang from the cracks of the pavement. This park, in the middle of Baltimore, had deer running around!

I had to climb out of the park and popped into a pretty nice neighborhood. You can usually tell by the presence of speed bumps. The fancy neighborhood did not last long though. Before I knew it, I was dodging cars blowing through red lights and fucked up people wandering into the street. People were walking around with blunts and non-bagged 40s shouting at cops. Cops were texting and driving. This place was like a third-world country. More houses were boarded up than occupied. The weird part was that there were mattresses everywhere. It all seemed like a big block party in Allston at first, so I just rolled with it. At one point I had to pee. I didn't do anything but pull over to the side of the road to "blend in". When in Rome.

Being in a big city, my GPS was sending me all over the place. I needed to find Route 1, the artery of the city, and that would get me out of this Gotham-like place. After a dozen missed turns and nearly getting right hooked by Chryslers, I found it by nothing more than a stroke of luck and started moving. The epicenter of the city, the financial area that always has the tall buildings, passed in the blink of an eye. The area now was getting back to the outer layers which were just getting worse and worse. I was moving along but getting held up at a lot of red lights. To avoid any interaction, I tried not to look at anyone, let alone make eye contact. I came to a stop light at four-way intersection with a liquor store on the corner. That's when a group of dudes paid particular attention to the neon-blinking madness that I was. "Let's go get that bike, boys!" one said as they start heading towards me. I took off like a track sprinter and even burned the cars next to me for a couple blocks. No time for traffic lights now! Nervous and shaken, I started laughing. I thought, *I can't believe that just happened*. My spirits lifted as Route 1 turned into highway, bringing me out of that hellhole.

Even though the highway was an improvement, the road looked like it had been under construction for years. The city clearly had no money for anything. It was sad. These abandoned projects clearly had impact on the community. No wonder why there were so many human rights issues here. It was plain to see that many of these people had nothing. The highway was strewn with abandoned, stripped vehicles. There were more cars on blocks with smashed windows than ones that would pass inspection. Debris was everywhere. Glass, nails, truck tires, and huge swaths of metal littered my path. I had to keep swerving from the one open lane into equally dangerous construction. Meanwhile, my lights were slowly dying one by one. My laughter quickly spun into a state of complete disarray. This road I was on was bad. This kind of highway traffic usually doesn't get to me, but this time I could not hang. Now it was 10:30, and I still had over forty miles to go. Those would mostly be through Washington, D.C. and would run me passed midnight. That was something I did not want to have to go through again.

My friend Lynn had set me up with a couple, Mary and Rod, who were going to help me get through D.C. They had picked up some stuff from CVS for me earlier in the day and were even going to pump up my tires. I gave Mary a call. My breath hung in the air, sitting on the edge of the highway. She answered, and I just went straight into it: "Is there any way I could stay at your place tonight? I really don't need anything, I can just curl up on the floor somewhere." Right away and enthusiastically, Mary told me yes. God bless this woman. There was about fifteen miles to crank out before meeting them. For some reason, in a state of panic, I decided to eat the Chipotle burrito from my jersey pocket in three bites. Not a suggested form of ingestion, by the way.

When I rode cross country people would let me stay at their place. A lot even went out of their way to offer me a bed. The kindness of strangers is a real thing. Before I take off on an adventure, I'm always asked the same dumb question: "Are you going to bring a gun?" To which I always give the oh-so-cool and witty response: "That's just extra weight." That's the problem with our twenty-four-hour news cycle of fear mongering. Everything is spun into fear and danger to keep you hooked and their ratings up. When you take even one minute to talk to 99% of people, you realize how much they want to help.

I met up with Rod on the way to their place. He came ripping out of the darkness like a knight storming a castle. I noticed that he had quite the sweet rig when he pulled up. His rear-hub was loud and screamed to the night sky. His bike had all the fixings that a long-distance cyclist would gawk at. Right away I clearly recognized a dude who rides many miles. I kept trying to crack him with questions of riding until we met up with Mary. She was bubbly and well-lit as she rolled up to Rod and me. She was like an angel emerging from the darkness to accompany my new knight-pal Rod and me through the night. It was great to ride with some company.

Mary told me there were people waiting for me up the road. "Me?" I asked; I was shocked. Right then, cheers omitted from the darkness. A couple who were a big part of the D.C. cycling scene were waiting in the middle of the night for me just to pass by. It gave me goosebumps. We took the next right and there was another friend with a sign for me that read "GO BICYCLE BRENDAN!" written in glow sticks and glitter. She told me NAMI had done so much for her. I stopped and snapped a quick picture before the last couple blocks to Mary and Rod's place.

When I got there, Mary and Rod offered me everything and more. She listed a list longer than a CVS receipt: beer, Gatorade, rice and beans, seltzer, anything that her kind and thoughtful soul could offer. Mary kept warming up plate after plate of rice and beans while roasting up what seemed like half a loaf of bread.

I was trying to eat until my eyes swelled up. She gave me a fizzy beverage and I just crammed down more. There was a mixture of excitement and fear in the eyes watching me eat like a wild animal. We chatted for a couple minutes, which my soul really needed. When you are flying, not stopping for more than fifteen minutes at a time, you don't really get to interact with people. These people meant everything to me at this point, and I was so grateful and happy to be a blip in their life.

Mary showed me where I would stay and told me to get some rest, only after telling me they were going to make breakfast and that Rod would ride with me. Divine! I washed my shorts in the bathroom sink and tossed them in the dryer for the morning. She let me use her office, where I plugged in all one million of my lights and gadgets to charge and prepped gear for the morning. The door was cracked, and her cat slipped in. Just like that, I felt normal again and passed out with her cat cuddled up with me like I would at home. I was able to relax for the first time in days. With my own bed and a cat by my side, I could've been back in Boston.

Hyattsville, MD to Roanoke Rapids, NC

I WOKE UP AT 5:30 the next morning after a solid night's rest. Sleep was very broken between visiting the bathroom and waking up in a pool of sweat every hour, but the comradery added a few extra hours to my REM cycle. When I went downstairs, Mary had granola, toast and fruit waiting for me. The three of us drank some primo French press coffee that was like diesel. Its dark, thick, velvety texture made me think of soft and easy morning making pancakes with Olyvia. I ate as much as I could while simultaneously getting my stuff together to beat first light. Since I eat a plant-based diet and Mary only had diary milk, I added water to my granola, which was divine. This deceiving concoction was hydrating and would fuel a big day ahead of me. Bless Mary's heart who seemed to feel bad about the water, but I actually felt ready to tackle the day today. I was set to ride through D.C. with Rod this morning. He had been a bike messenger in the city for over thirty years and now works on bikes in their bike share system. I couldn't ask for a better host and guide through the our nation's capital.

Early morning in D.C. was like everywhere else I've been. There were only two kinds of people outside right now chasing a fix, either trying to get their endorphins or a darker variety. We rode past the Capitol at sunrise as purple and orange hues warmed the city. The sun's exit after a cold fall night brought on the same warm beauty this morning. Weaving through morning road construction, there were stretches of tents under overpasses. It felt so strange in a place filled with millionaires and billionaires. The winding bike path through these nylon cities eventually led to Lafayette Square where my first desperate bathroom call was needed. I scrambled to a paperless port-a-potty only to have to go to the next. It seemed like everyone was an ultra-runner in this town. Geared up in their neon hydration vests and belts they came in huge waves. Two were there before me and confirmed my desperate toilet paper needs. Thank you, fellow endorphin addicts!

We made great timing for riding through a city. I would've

been extremely lost and wasted so much time. This was easily my biggest flaw as an adventurer. I was so glad to have Rod as my spirit guide through the capital. Chasing him was like a peyote trip where I followed an orange fox through a maze. We quickly found ourselves on the outskirts of the city heading due south to Virginia. I was so grateful to Rod for wanting to help me out that I kept asking him questions until he let me in a little bit, which led me to learn how similar we are in character. A fellow Dead Head (love me some Grateful Dead), he shared stories of shows come and gone that I could've only imagined. His tales from the shows in upstate New York combined with his wisdom of time was something I hoped to have. After talking for a while, he then told me that he was going to ride with me for a couple hours. Not only did I get help through a massively stressful situation twice in less than twenty-four hours, it would also be a huge relief to spend some time with another cyclist.

We went through a rolling state park of hills and abruptly turned to Jefferson Davis Highway and we started moving. It always takes me a few hours to warm up, especially as I get further into a project of this magnitude. This was your average American four-lane road with strip malls and big intersections. These are generally not the best places to cycle, but they are fast. When you're flowing with traffic it helps when said traffic is fast and angry. I could tell that Rod wanted to show me a nicer route away from all this, but he understood my situation and graciously came with me.

After about an hour of rush hour traffic and dodging 60-mph car mirrors, Rod was ready to turn around. We pulled over around mile thirty-five of the day, just on the crest of the woods by an Audubon Sanctuary. After a quick selfie, it was good-bye to my new friend. I can't thank him and Mary enough for everything they did for me after that night through Baltimore. They are both shining examples of the human spirit and I am so grateful to exist on Earth the same time they do.

I kept charging forward to Virginia. Strength in numbers had disappeared and I was on my own again. I was focused on short stops and few of them; no way would there be any precious time wasted away on a day set to be 210 miles. After Rod left, the traffic got worse before it got better. A few gigantic trucks zipped past my head honking and yelling; there's no way to console a "small" man, if you know what I'm saying.

I was looking for lunch when I found a Trek store just up ahead. I knew I needed gloves after the toll my hands had taken the past days without them. They were alternating between that dull ache and actually hurting. I went in, made a beeline to the gloves, and bought the most cushioned pair they had. The employees asked why I was in such a rush and were elated by my story. My stop for gloves became even more apparent when I had to ask for help to take them out of the packaging. I had no fine motor skills in my hands to manipulate anything. One of the employees, a new friend and aspirational do-gooder, Luis, helped me get that damn package open so I could get back on the road. With a new set of gloves, it was back to Jefferson Davis and into Virginia.

The double-laned highway looked just like the rest of suburban America. Except the people here especially didn't like cyclists on their road. Big trucks would "coal roll" me, emptying exhaust fumes in a plume of smog temporarily suffocating and blinding me. Pretty much the exact kind of road that you don't want to ride a bike on. I'm sure engineers designed this whole infrastructure concept without bikes in mind. This wasn't about to stop me though. If anything, I was speeding up with the traffic. I couldn't do any of my normal commuting tricks because of my aching mitts, but it hardly messed with my progress. Honestly, I think the cars were more afraid of me for some reason. Probably because I looked like a lunatic, who has nothing on their side but confidence and blind fucking ignorance.

Around mile sixty-five it was time for first lunch, so I of course, opted to "Eat Fresh". Being plant-based, I'm always finding little tricks to add calories to my diet but also save time. Years ago, I used to manage a sandwich shop in Boston. I smoked more pot and drank more beers in that place than we made sandwiches, which is saying a lot, since this was the #1-rated sandwich shop in the city. I pulled an old trick from those days of blackout nights and stoned mornings. At the end of the line of food protective glass, I had them make me a foot-long veggie and crush a bag of chips on it. This would get me some of the calories that I desperately needed and some sodium to get me through the rising heat of the day. As they were assembling the sandwich and wrapping it into separate halves for me, I chugged a Gatorade and put another on my bike. I was starting to figure stuff out a little bit. No time could be wasted. Seconds add up to minutes and minutes add up to hours, which quickly, turn into a days.

Back on the road with a sub in my stomach and another in my back pocket, I was ready to crush some more miles. The scenery was thickening with more defining characteristics, I was really beginning to feel like I was in the south. The earth was turning red with clay and the trucks were getting bigger and bigger. Beat up pickup trucks with large smokestacks and dual rear wheels. The kind where they clearly used them for farm work and not for overcompensating. The road was pancake flat and I had an excellent tail wind as I was coasting down the road. I was moving along, and people were reaching out about my progress. Prior to the start of the ride, I uploaded my entire route into an interactive map so people could follow along on my website during the trip. Thanks to yesterday's Havre De Grace bridge fiasco and near robbery, my route had changed drastically. With no choice but to look forward, the route did make a lot more logistical sense than before. This was a much-needed confidence boost. For once, I felt like I could fall into a bit of a groove.

I tucked into my aero bars and got to work. My stomach was giving me some issues, but I managed only one roadside stop. This was the best possible scenario I could've found myself in. I was scouring Google Maps for a restaurant I could pop into to do the deed. I have no problem being the proverbial bear in the woods, but a commercially cleaned bathroom has its perks. Since this is really a battle of sustaining more than anything, hygiene was a priority. Not the dirt kind, but the yo-that's-actually-nasty-dude kind of hygiene. Wash your damn hands, kids.

I pushed on all the way to Richmond to get my food drop at the Red Roof Inn where I had originally planned on staying the previous night. Whenever I'm out on the road, I always seem to roll through towns when something is going on. Coming into Richmond was a huge relief, unlike every other city in history. Like usual, the buildings were messing up my phone and Garmin GPS readings, but as far as cities go, it's actually very easy to navigate. There was a big festival covering the entire city. Music echoed through the streets, down alleys and main ways. People were crisscrossing the streets all over town and I loved it. This place was alive, like a beehive.

My food drop went perfectly and was adjacent to another Subway. I hadn't planned on grabbing food, but logistically it made a lot of sense. I ate the old half that was still kicking in my jersey pocket and refilled my snack set up. Chocolatey snacks in the left food bag and fruity on the right. I could fit a few thousand calories just up front. Combined with what I had fit into my seat pack, I was working out a great way to haul calories at a relatively low cost, both in money and in weight. I had a pretty heavy-duty plastic bag filled with snacks, which I bungeed along with my rain gear down to the pack. I still had those yellow dish gloves from New York and was now using them as makeshift reflectors. The missing fingers would flap around in the wind, waving to passersby as they drove passed me at light speed.

Following in the success of my previous food stop with another 6-inch for the road, bike math was starting to look positive for the first time. I began to follow my Garmin which led me straight to the gates of DuPont, the chemical manufacturer. There were trails all behind that massive cohort of smokestacks and factory buildings that my Garmin and Google were telling me to take. I went into security armed with my best smile and asked the guard if she would let me through. "Just one exception, Miss?" I tried but simply got a resounding "NO," citing that it was too dangerous. Given her post, she must have not seen anyone for a while, especially a man. She was like a junkyard dog, drooling over a juicy steak and was dying to conversate. I asked where Jefferson Davis Highway was, and her eyes grew to the size of dinner plates. She said, "Oh lord, you don't want to ride a bike on that. It is far too dangerous, honey." I did, in fact, want to ride on that road, nice lady. It was my only option.

This was looking to be my first day that I would break 200 miles while finishing before midnight. I just needed to keep my pace to make sure of it. The road was undulating over the southern Virginia hills which suited my riding style quite well. I rolled into the last town of the state and felt a strange excitement. Cars on cinderblocks and guys with huge home stereos on their lawn playing music for the whole block. The energy here was palpable and someone nearly hit me as I took a sharp right. He was enraged and started screaming at me, "Do you wanna fucking die, boy?!" That was not my intention and I certainly had no time for this mad man. I apologized and got out of town as quickly as possible.

The sun was beginning to set, and I had to plan my nightly food delivery to my hotel. It must have been a pretty hilarious sight. A disheveled guy in the middle of Nowhere, Virginia yelling into his phone on speaker ordering a pizza. I can only imagine the people who passed me told their side of the story to their local friends. "Out of nowhere there was this crazy guy on a bike. He was mangy with long hair and a grizzly beard, I think he really needed a pizza."

Meanwhile, Olyvia was at her best friend's wedding as the maid of honor. Before I left, I knew I was going to miss it and felt awful. Not only for our friends Bri and Ben, but I wanted to support my loving wife who always has my back. When I realized that I couldn't be there, I wrote a message to Bri on Facebook. I told her about how bad I felt about missing it. She told me it wasn't my fault that I was hit by a car earlier in the year. Every day I had been uploading an update video to my Facebook page so everyone could follow along. Today, I had a special shoutout to the new McDonald family. I'm still sorry I missed your special day, guys. I love you both.

If not for the change of pavement at the state line, crossing into North Carolina could have gone completely unnoticed to the untrained eye. It was a heartfelt moment for me, surrounded in the warm beauty of the south. My voice floated across the sunset soaked cotton field that filled the horizon as a train seemingly floated south alongside me. You could almost taste the sweet tea in the air coming from huge houses with wrap-around porches.

There were only forty miles or so left on the day when I stopped at a huge gas station for water. It sat alone on the intersection at the last main road heading out of the sleepy town I was passing through. Its powerful lights and neon sign lit the sky amongst a sea of darkness and trees. It felt like the modern crossroads where people would come for miles to trade their goods. Though I was tempted by Subway once again, I opted simply for the Ferrari water, aka Smartwater. There were more than enough calories in my bags to get me to Roanoke Rapids where I would rest my weary head tonight.

The highway was dark and desolate as it wound through rural North Carolina. Strange, long, twisty ramps brought me from one side to another over crossing highways. Luckily, it was the only road out here, so my chances of getting lost were low. Also, since it was fully dark, I could see any cars coming even before they saw all five of my taillights. The road heightened how alone I was out here and made me reflect on the love of my friends. Olyvia at Bri's wedding, Mike working on his film work and my two oldest friends just moving into an apartment together in a big city. My love for them filled the night around me and their joint successes made my heart swell with pride.

As all these thoughts were running through my mind, suddenly, I desperately needed to go to the bathroom. There was no room for error in my decision-making if you know what I mean. By some strange stroke of luck, there was a small gas station I barely made it to. It serendipitously coincided with a strange need for Welch's fruit snacks. It was not time to question clean eating or childhood snack urges; it was time to indulge both my cavities and my inner child. Two women at the counter were chatting about their potential lottery winnings and asked me the question. Their southern charm and air-conditioned store lent me to tell them my story. Their wishes of safe travels warmed my heart, and I wished them much luck on their future lottery success.

The temporary relief didn't last long though as I could not wait and found the next gas station... and then the next... and then the next... These stops were eating up all my time that I had so preciously gained. But the road here was perfect. Its large berth lent me plenty of space to relax and lean into the peddles as I tried to stretch out the nerves in my hands. Their shape was starting to curl in more and more at the ring and pinky fingers. Soon, the highway ended and I got pretty lost on some dead-end dirt roads, making an uncomfortable ride even more excruciating. I truly felt like I was going to explode now. It felt like my stomach bubbled from my toes up to my ears while I squirmed in agony, praying to find another bathroom. It was unbearably frustrating when I had to stop at a gas station only a few miles away from my hotel. There was no more time. I made it in there with all the subtlety of a steamboat. Unfortunately, I didn't make it there quite in time...

I left the gas station both relieved and depressed. The embarrassment of the '90s Nickelodeon cartoon sounds omitting from the bathroom caught everyone's attention in the store, but I had no shame. Nature was the one making the calls; I was just trying my best to answer. Just as I left the fluorescent lights of the Shell station, I got a call from my Domino's delivery driver. He had been at the Red Roof Inn where I was staying. "You have 5 minutes," he said. I tried telling him I rode my bike there from Maryland and just to leave the pizza. This was completely out of the realm of perception for this guy, who really follows the rules apparently. I went full sprint for the last three miles, passing cars and slipping through late-night traffic to make it just in time. The air hung with humidity and the scent of a commercial pig farm nearby, which really seemed to set the stage for the scenery.

With a massive effort, I made it to the hotel and found General Domino's still there waiting for me. Though I was pretty pissed at this guy's total lack of awareness, I made sure to be as nice as possible to him. Truthfully, I just wanted my food and would've robbed him in the parking lot for that damn pizza if necessary. The front desk was staffed by a woman named Crystal. Her classic, caring, southern charm made her a great person to ring you in at midnight after riding 211 miles. She was enthusiastic about the adventure and willing to help as my phone blew up. It was like everyone was calling and texting me all at once. I couldn't help but be flustered as I was trying to end my night. "You should turn that thing off," she said. "You need to focus on your rest, honey." I've always liked being called honey. I told her I liked that people were thinking about and looking out for me. Even with mixed emotions, it's important not to forget people care about you more than you realize in those dark times.

I settled in for the night after racing through all my chores. Multi-tasking was a key move to get to bed earlier at night. Because there is only one way to get a vegan pizza at Domino's,

I was on the thin crust bandwagon. My ingenuity here was invaluable as I came up to the optimum solution this time. I took that once crispy, now slightly flaccid disc and folded it over to a calzone. Double slices, baby. This was by far the most successful day I'd had so far, even with the bathroom issues at the end. I had crushed 211 miles before midnight and went through all of Virginia in a day. Going to sleep, I felt proud and worthy of the day's efforts.

ROANOKE RAPIDS, NC TO DILLON, SC

I T WAS A far rougher morning than I expected. Feeling somewhere between a nasty hangover and the flu, I was a shell of a man. My head was 1000 degrees. My clothes were still soaking wet from last night, so I wore nothing but rain pants and tossed them in the hotel dryer. To my surprise, Crystal was still holding down the front desk. Granted, it had only been about five hours and I'm sure she puts in long shifts. I hit up the continental breakfast, and after half a dozen cups of orange juice I was back at it. It was the first warm morning, and I had to strip layers off right away. I wasn't used to the environment of the south, no idea whatsoever of how mornings warm with the sun. When I pulled over, a van came screeching to a halt. I had jumped a no-trespassing fence to take care of some of that hummingbird food called orange juice. With my heart in my throat, I looked up to find a guy just looking out for me. He told me there aren't many cyclists out here and wanted to help if I needed it. I didn't need that info to put all of this together.

After town, there were cotton fields everywhere, miles and miles as far as the eye could see. Plot after plot was packed with white tufts from boundary line to boundary line. The houses were little more than dilapidated shacks with holes in the roof situated at the ends of dirt driveways. Broken frames of homes long ago consumed by vines along the road's edge. The strangest part was that most had brand new Dodge Chargers in the driveway. The only people I saw were two kids, no older than seven, playing in the driveway. One yelled "Hey, white man! Give us some money!" I started to feel so awful about the state of affairs in this area and that I couldn't give those kids more than a smile and a peace sign. A wave of emotions came crashing down on me. I couldn't fathom the lives these kids must lead, such an extreme contrast of what I had experienced in my youth.

I grew up in the lower end of middle class, always had a roof over my head and food to eat. I called my mother and told her how grateful I was for all they did for me. There were five kids in the house, and I came in eight years younger than my closest sibling. The neighborhood was filled with houses that were formally small cabins, families packed inside like cigarette-flavored sardines. The kids of the neighborhood all hung out just like The Sandlot: fights over packs of candy cigarettes, football games, and shooting each other with BB guns until the sun set. Most people don't see the places you visit during bicycle travel. They go to the city centers and tourists traps and claim they've "been there", but it's not until you smell the shit people live in until you can truly understand. My heart was heavy for them.

What happened next is like a re-occurring nightmare happening in slow motion. I was trying to decide on my first food stop of the day. With my new system I was able to search along the route a little better and quickly became paralyzed by the options. Without realizing it, I blew through a stop sign. A beat-up Chrysler did the same thing and didn't slow down a bit. I looked up from my phone just in time to see the car come within inches of my front tire. If either of us were any bit faster, the result would have been catastrophic. My suspense held in the air. I couldn't breathe. I thanked every god that I was alive. That I could keep riding. Any point of contact from that collision would've totaled my bike. I made a vow then to make safety a priority.

After a few hours of pedaling I ended up at the Subway in Nashville, North Carolina. The sandwich with chips and guac special. Sitting down, I quickly ate the entire footlong like a dog who has been begging for food. I should've been wearing a snorkel so some oxygen could have gotten into my lungs. As I was packing up, I had to go to the bathroom twice. Thinking nothing of it, I grabbed my stuff and moved on to the second objective. I went next door to the Dollar General to feed my peanut butter craving. There was something deep inside me, at the bone marrow level or DNA even, that craved that salty, fatty goodness. Normally, I am quite the connoisseur of nut butters. Only the simplest of ingredients and care will suffice for my upper echelon pallet. But, for now, the double palm-oil special would have to be a place holder. The cashier gave me a plastic knife and I had the brilliant idea to try and snap a piece off so I could leave it stuffed in the jar. My precise snap was anything short of accurate, and I was left with a plastic nub to deliver the goods. I was just happy not to have to use my grubby fingers.

Soon after getting back on the road, I had to go to the bathroom again. I quickly realized something was wrong, but I couldn't figure out how to fix it. I had to make my rounds with people who could offer some solution. Like a mirage appearing in the desert sands of the Sahara, a real Mexican convenience store in the middle of North Carolina. The interior had a pool table, funky hats, corny t-shirts with poor grammar on the front, the kind you need to buy just to cut the sleeves off. I smiled at the cashier when I walked in and quickly found the bathroom against the far wall. Without comparison, this bathroom was easily one of the most unique places I've been. I guess I can thank this sudden stomach ailment to my strange luck. The "room" was this not-quite-walled space with a toilet and a sink. It had no light fixture above at all. I felt terrible and actually embarrassed as I used all their toilet paper. Without choice, I did the right thing and left the empty roll on top of the seat (don't be an inconsiderate monster now, people), thanked the laughing cashier, and left. I'm sure the sweaty biker was a hit story with all her customers that day.

Right when I was back on the bike, I called all the female figures I knew would answer, hoping one of them could recommend something to help me. First, my mom who never answers at work miraculously answered. Then I called Olyvia who was dealing with "the wine flu", today being the day after her best friend's wedding. She even consulted her mom after we hung up. Then I called my sister, Sarah, who is both a chiropractor and nutritionist. I was in full-on crisis response mode. Something like this could really end my trip, let alone completely trash my chances on setting the record. Not only was it taking a toll on my body through dehydration, but it was also taking up an immense amount of time. With all their help, we collectively came up with a solution. Even if this was just a metaphorical Band-aid, it would help. The next town I'd stop in, I'd grab probiotics and Pepto-Bismol and take them both. It wasn't until I called Olyvia back to tell her the story of my mom and me ordering pizza last night that I realized one of my mistakes. Only one of the sauces at Domino's is lactose free and, needless to say, we didn't put that together correctly last night. Thank god for the reliable, quick-thinking women in my life. While my diet needed a re-vamp, there was at least now a known cause for the action.

Moving a little faster now as I appeared to squeeze the poison out of me, I was making progress. As I drudged down the road in the mid-day heat, I saw more dogs in cages then I ever have in my life. They we confined in the tiniest of spaces, clearly trotting the same pattern over and over a thousand times a day. Many had worn huge paths of dirt below sea level in their small plots of overgrown grass. The rusty chains rattled as the dogs snapped at me when I rode past. What I was witnessing was a life of confinement, negligent owners without regard for life. There was no imagining the pain and suffering these animals endured or why they were there in the first place. I wanted to save them all. One of my life goals is to help animals of all species become liberated from the chains of humanity. We take and take and take, not only from other humans, but especially animals.

Just then, as I popped over the crest of a ditch shaped hill, I saw my first cyclist. A true triathlete looking dude. Equipped with the aero helmet and all, he zipped past me like he didn't see me. As if he didn't just pass the most standout character he could've possibly crossed paths with in this area who also happened to be on a bike. I gave him a friendly "Hey, man!" to which he ever so kindly offered a coy, "Hey." I was a little salty about it. Every part of me just wanted to say, "Fuck you, guy!" in true Bostonian fashion but just kept rolling. I've been there, hammering away, laser focused on the road while training for an Iron Man too. I would've said more than a brush off though. To all cyclists: please be nicer to everybody and people might start acting like we *don't deserve to die*. Sincerely, a guy who no longer wants to die.

Just after my salty encounter, I was starting to feel ill. A wave of nausea crashed over and soaked me. I was getting delirious. I unzipped my jersey and was wobbling around the road, just managing to dodge the lifted pick-up trucks that came barreling down the road. I pulled my head back up and made eye contact with a passing cyclist. He saw the despair in my eyes and shouted, "You're looking good, buddy!" His words and timing were world class and made me start to snap out of it. Eventually I realized that I hadn't accounted for the southern heat in my fluid intake and had been drinking water like I was still in Maine. I started drinking as much as I could without wasting it. Your kidneys can really only handle a few gulps every fifteen or so minutes. Using some bike math, I realized I had the perfect amount of fluids to get to the next CVS. I instantly began to feel better and dumped the rest of that bottle over my head. The gritty, salty sweat rolled down my head into my beard and hardened.

I drank a over two liters of water in less than two hours as I made my way to the CVS and started to feel alive again. Coming into Smithfield was such a sweet relief. There were actual services here and what seemed like an entire community watching the town's little league baseball. When I got into the town center, I raided their CVS. To compensate for all the lost electrolytes, I slammed Body Armor after Body Armor, standing right in front of the entrance where the A/C was cranking. The cool air would've brought goosebumps to my skin if my blood wasn't a degree below boiling. I took two armfuls of the biggest bottles of coconut water and Gatorade to the counter. All those electrolytes in combination with Pepto and a probiotic brought me back to life. My body temperature started to regulate a bit when I soaked my entire head in their bathroom sink. I watched the spiraling swirl of the sweat and road grime descend into their plumbing. Now cooled off with freshly re-applied sunscreen, it was time to start cranking again.

I was now on course for Fayetteville and was making decent progress. The roads between these two towns were horrible, like they started to do roadwork and grade the pavement but then left and never came back. It was oddly exhausting for my legs and exacerbated the dull ache of my hands as I tried to lightly grip my bars. The only thing I could do was take long, slow deep breaths to relax so I could let this obstacle pass. It was a strange test of mental fortitude. There were no alternatives. The fastest way is always through.

Even though the fluids and Pepto were doing the trick, it was time to try to change up my diet a little. Everyone I spoke with suggested it, but there isn't much you can do in this scenario. You are dependent on gas station snacks, quick takeout food, and the occasional well-timed pickup order. A couple hours after my stomach-saving trip to CVS, I made it to Fayetteville. This was a beautiful, charming southern town from the moment I got into it. The town center had elegant store fronts and streets made of brick, which is a seriously double-edged sword when you're riding a bike, but after the miles of vibrating farm road,

I took it with open arms. One of my food drops was at a hotel on the edge of town next to the strip mall restaurants that I would normally avoid. I was dead set on getting a burrito for some reason. Just like my earlier peanut butter desire, I wasn't about to question what I needed. A sit-down chain was my only offering for the Mexican delight. The gentleman at the front desk was very confused about my mobile-ritto needs. There was no time to waste, so as my order went to the kitchen, I went dashing across town to the hotel for my pickup. Re-supplied with snacks, I made sure to grab some more Ferrari water on my way back to my pickup. The cashier was a kind, middle-aged woman with a huge pistol on her hip. It was most definitely the South down here. I said, "Thank you, ma'am," while slowly leaving with my hands visible to avoid an unnecessary .45 to the back. It was just starting to get dark when I got back for my food. To call this thing a "burrito" would be a flat out lie. The greasy, flat mess sat stagnant in an aluminum dish with a sack of tortilla chips on the side. With the enlisted help of the kitchen staff, I was able to make it more portable, all while sucking down as many chips as possible like a vacuum. On the way out, I gave my chips to a nice elderly couple who were simply thankful and not weary of my intentions. The southern charm warmed my heart, and I was grateful to have a moment here.

The last shift of the day was about to be underway, and I still had over sixty miles to go, none of which were set to be on favorable cycling roads. In an effort to take away a bit of the anxiety, I had to make one last bathroom break, just in case. Cutting tight corners at red lights, I passed every chain restaurant in existence. I held out until the very last gas station before hitting the dark North Carolina highway. It was busy and people were moving in and out of the place like carpenter ants. There was no time to question it. I wheeled the bike in, turned my lights off, and leaned it against the cases of water in front of the solo bathroom. To save time and the inevitable disaster that sloppy burrito would make, I ate it while going to the bathroom. Never an ideal situation to eat a burrito in a bathroom, especially if you're sitting on the John. Leaving the last bit of artificial light for the night, I heard the sarcastic cashier comment, "Yeah, it's totally cool to bring your bike inside." I smiled and said thanks before heading into the now pitch-black countryside.

The streetlights ended almost immediately, leaving me to navigate roads lined with slaughterhouses and not built for bicycles in the dark. The shoulder was eight inches at its widest with 18 wheelers to my left and sand to my right. Their symphony of rubber barreling down the road was like the whistling sound of bombs falling. *I better hold this damn line*, I thought. This was also not helping my tunnel-visioned state. I was so behind on sleep that having to focus on the line made me feel like I was wearing drunk goggles. This was also the first time I turned all my lights on. Before, I'd tier them, turning on one at a time to ensure that their batteries lasted. Given the state, I figured that being "safe" in this scenario was an obvious reason to turn them on. With the one remaining handlebar plug light (after losing the other twenty miles out on the first day) and four taillights flashing in erratic, dancehall patterns, I was my own two-wheeled disco partying down a narrow line of madness.

The cool air left a lofty feeling beneath me as I pushed heavy on the peddles. My late-night urge for candy struck once again, and I crunched away at my supply, finishing off those hard candies that I still had stashed from Connecticut. Their sugary goodness kept my mind occupied and kept filling me with glycogen. I was actually going pretty quickly now! This was quickly becoming one of my favorite things. It was now around 10:30 and there were already way fewer cars on the road. Since it wasn't too late, they hopefully weren't too drunk yet. I passed small parties of highway homes as I zipped along on the -1% grade.

In no time, an hour disappeared beneath the rubber of my Continentals and I started to see signs for South Carolina. Not long after, I could see an ominous glow illuminating the dark horizon. My grip loosened and a smile creeped out of my soul in excitement. As I came around the bend, there was Dillon, South Carolina's Vegas. The entire town was a fluorescent and neon display. There were giant neon dinosaurs and leprechauns overlooking this now quiet strip. My daily odometer was just a smidge under 207 miles while rolling up to the hotel for the night. When I tried to check in, the woman at the front desk laughed and told me I was next door. I was at the wrong hotel, which, in my defense had an almost identical name. I hopped the ledge, crashed through some bushes, and just tipped the mileage scale to 207 for the day.

I was ready for a proper meal and rest. I got at least half of that. With another night of Domino's, nutrition was about to be fixed. Hell, I drank a soda for the first time in years and my stomach felt great from its bubbly goodness. A sandwich, a large pizza, and a Sprite later, I cleaned my bike and passed out.

DILLON, SC TO BEAUFORT, SC

TODAY WAS GOING to be a big day! WPOR from Portland, Maine was scheduled to interview me early this morning, and South Carolina was the first state I would be in for more than a day since Maine. Things were lining up to be a great day in the saddle. *Maybe I'll be able to get in early tonight*, I thought as I rolled out of the hotel parking lot.

It was great being on flatter terrain. My average speed increased ever so slightly, which builds up fast. Minutes turn miles, and I was cutting time off quickly. I met a gentleman outside my morning bathroom stop in Lotta. I decided to shoot my first "Where are we?" video, something I wish I'd thought of sooner. I simply asked, "What's your name and where are we?" I added in some of my colorful humor. He was excited to be on camera but didn't seem as excited about my adventure. Thanks for the help regardless, buddy!

My interview was early in the morning and was scheduled to air later in the day. Until this point of the ride, I had been yelling through speaker phone completely unaware that people only heard a third of the conversation. So after a test call with my headphones in, I was ready to tell my story. They gave me some softball questions and gave the classic "I don't even like to drive that far!" but this didn't help with how nervous I secretly felt. I had never been on the radio other than to request AC/DC when I was ten. Those questions are still up on SoundCloud somewhere. After the interview aired, I got $500 for the charity in no time. I am so grateful to John, Joe, and Courtney for their help in spreading the message. Give those guys at WPOR some support for having their hearts in the right place.

The interview lit a flame inside me, and I was cranking now, averaging 17 mph, a blazing speed for ultra-cycling, and made my lunch stop as clouds began to set it. I tried to be quick with my "half for here, half for the road" procedure, but a kind nurse asked me where I got my shoes. It might have been my spandex that she was really looking at, but I laughed and told her they wouldn't be good for spending hours on her feet.

The forecast said rain, but my optimism said no. Unfortunately, Mother Nature doesn't give a shit what you think. Before I knew it, I was in a serious southern downpour. The drops were fat and coming at me from every angle. I was fortunate enough that my route was paved most of the way. The highway I was on brought me through residential areas and not just the strip malls we see while travelling in a car. The rain began coming down so hard that a third of the highway flooded. The water forced me into the road, away from the shoulders, which were already covered in pieces of blown tires and quickly degrading into marshes of sand and overgrowth. I had to alternate between the lane and a middle space which was something between a lane and a median. It was way safer but seriously pissed some drivers off. When I tried to move back over to the shoulder to avoid confrontation with an armed madman, I was almost flattened by a minivan. This shook me up, and I had to take a moment to settle down and drink the warm Gatorade from my bottle cages in a graveyard.

I noticed I was going hard from both my heart rate and how hungry I was. I took it as my body saying, "I'm feeling good today." But subconsciously, I always push it when I'm nervous. I had to eat the other half of the sandwich that I was saving for later far earlier than I hoped. It was a little soggy after dangling from my handlebars in the downpour, but I liked the change from the two-a-day I had been eating.

The road grew busier each passing moment as it approached evening rush hour. My initial route had me going through Charleston, but now, with my new route, this would've added a solid fifteen miles. I held up for a bit to grab food from a gas station. Soon after I got back on the road, it finally stopped raining, the first time in six hours. I pulled over and took off my rain gear to air out. Somehow, in the process I managed to tear apart my legs on the prickly roadside vegetation. Another big "Fuck you" from this area, and with what felt like infinity hours before I'd stop in Beaufort for the night.

Next, it was time to grab more food at a nearby gas station before I started on my third and final shift of the day. Despite the sign outside, the Dunkin' Donuts inside was just a small island coffee bar in the middle of the convenience portion of their shop. At this point coffee just turned my insides out more than it gave me any sort of boost. I was a man who need some overcooked, soggy hash browns.

Making haste and grabbing as many Lenny and Larry's cookies as I could from the store, I was a little frustrated approaching the counter. Everything about me looked worse than a drowned and bloodied rat. After my conversation with the endlessly upbeat cashier, it was on to the actual Dunkin' Donuts. The inside was empty, and the place was staffed by teenagers on their first day. Somehow, they all seemed like they were training each other, just given keys to the store and told to figure it out as they went.

The time dragged by as I did as many tasks as I could occupy myself with while they buzzed and bumped around the back. I, for some ungodly reason, got an onion bagel, which I was planning to spread peanut butter on. When I went outside, excited to get moving after wasting almost forty-five minutes, it was raining again. I couldn't believe it. I had essentially wasted all the time I'd worked so hard for. Wasted energy. I put all my rain gear on and went back to the road with a bagel in my jersey pocket. I tried not to mull on my frustration too much and started to bob down an increasing line of traffic. The pace was good, so I was managing to float right up the side. A woman turned from a Jeep with no doors and blew a huge cloud of cigarette smoke on me. In a panic she apologized, and I just laughed at her honest accident. They most certainly don't have a lot of cyclists around here.

It was nice to be off the highway, but now it was an even smaller shoulder than the night before. There were about three inches I could feasibly ride on, and now it was full-blown rush hour. No one has a worse attitude than commuters. They're pissed from going to a job they hate only to spend hours driving to get home to a family they hopefully do actually like. A weird existence that we Americans live.

The spray from the cars was, in a way, keeping me cool while I was white knuckling my bars. No hope for tucking into the aerobars, this was absolutely a grip-and-hold-that-fucking-line scenario. Most cars were courteous, but there were the assholes. It seemed to be mostly truck drivers, smog dumping, nearly sideswiping, small-endowed truck drivers. They hardly kept to their own lane as they flew by on this razor thin back road.

These are the scenarios where nothing you do truly matters. There's only so much you can do once you're already in it; the rest is just left up to fate. The more you bring the fear and neg-ativity to your situation, the worse your perception is. You can be in a safe, warm, and well-lit room but be scared and lost in the dark pits of the mind. It's best to grab the bars with a clear intent and let those thoughts go.

I was scanning Google Maps when I noticed a road that would bring me back down to my original route and would save me five miles. I was willing to take any chance to get my feet out of the rain sooner. I banked left and started down a road with no traffic. It was quiet and it was saving time. Win, win! I blinked my eyes at the instant relief from the huge sensory explosion that was that state highway. After keeping to the road for a few miles, I saw a sign that said, "Pavement Ends". My heart plummeted to the molten crust of the earth's core. You might say that just adds to the adventure; you can also fuck right off. Nothing is worse than riding through quicksand on 28mm tires. The entire morning had already been turned upside down after avoiding just that for hours. I turned around and got absolutely pissed for the first time on the whole adventure. I started shouting and slamming my handlebars. The harder I slammed the pads on my handlebars, the angrier I got.

Have you ever noticed being around people who complain a lot tends to make you complain? Chronic complaining is a disease. Instead of trying to fix the situation or letting the emotion pass by, they latch on. Yelling about the thing that put them in this endless state of irritation. Poking the bruise never helps it heal. It's forward progress (and maybe a massage) that helps you move forward. Banging my hands was just adding to my pain and frustration, not "blowing off steam". It's better to not even grab hold of the anger than to have to try and let it go.

In the blink of an eye, my day went from 10:30 to midnight again. This was about to be another rule of the 10k: Every day ends at midnight. Since I chopped down my 220-mile days to 200-210, they had all ended at midnight. In this moment, it was something I simply had to accept instead of fight. No matter how far or how well the day was going at a particular time, I was ending at midnight. Once I accepted this simple fact, my night shift became increasingly more enjoyable.

There was one more town to pass through before the last long stretch of Route 17 to Beaufort. New habits were forming, and I had an insatiable craving for Jolly Ranchers. Since I ran out of my Connecticut candies, I needed some more midnight sugar. I stopped at the last gas station before the hard line of the town's final streetlight gave way to darkness.

I pulled up to the gas station, flashing like am ambulance with all seven of my lights on, and went inside for more Ferrari water and information. After being skunked on my last attempt, I wasn't about to have this happen again. I asked the person at the cash register if the road right next to them was paved and he said he didn't understand. I went and checked the bathroom really quick to empty out the tank. Occupied. There was a gentleman stocking the nearby cooler while I waited, so I asked him. "What do you mean?" he snarled, "They just paved this road!"

I usually try to de-inflate, not just de-escalate, people like this. Angry for some other reason, but I happened to be the one who crossed his path. People are almost never taking out their anger on the thing that actually caused their frustration. Most people will bottle it up and dump it all over someone else later. Usually, we do this to the people we care the most about.

This man and I had never met before, so I decided to try again. "That's great! This road has been good—" absolute, crock-of-shit lie "—But I got stuck on a dirt road by mistake and I have really skinny tires. I'm just trying to avoid riding my bicycle through that again. Is Route 211 paved for bicycles?" He looked shocked that I was riding a bike at all, let alone at this time of night. "Yeah, it's paved," he replied as I shook the bathroom door handle for the twelfth time.

After my Jolly-Rancher-bathroom-information shakedown, I was back on the road. Gazing up at a sky that had done nothing for me today left me unsure about my rain gear. I was so wet, not damp. My pants were floppy and saggy, same with my jacket. My shoes and feet were something I didn't even want to think about. Tired and worn, I was skiing down this alternating 2%

grade. It was now that time of night again where normal people are at home watching TV and the drunks aren't trying to drive home yet. I passed the time by trying to find the best Jolly Rancher combos. I would blindly stuff entire wrapped candies into my mouth and undo them with my tongue before guessing the color. The best combo is red and blue, if you're wondering.

I couldn't believe the exhausted state I was in. It was already after 11:30, and the hours of hard wet rain and a way-too-fast pace left me with truly nothing in the tank for the first time. I was desperate to get to the hotel, but no matter how hard I thought I was pushing, I couldn't seem to get above 13 mph. It felt like running in water.

The air was sweet as I looked out across the moonlit bay. The rain had stopped, but there was no way that I was going to be able to keep going until I reached the hotel. I was lost on another poorly labeled bike path and still a mile away from my hotel. I called Olyvia and said, "I have no idea how I could possibly ride tomorrow. I can't handle another day pushing it that hard. I think I just ruined the entire ride by one stupid day of rainy highway." I was ready for the whole thing to be done already. In her trademark stoicism, she simply replied, "You have to try."

She was right. After what felt like an eternity, I finally pulled up to my hotel. My rear hub screamed underneath the awning as

I walked in, always pulling all the attention. Looking around, I found a man sitting in the lobby with the concierge. With great enthusiasm, he gave me the "What the hell are you doing?" There was nothing left in me, but I felt the need to talk to him. I told him about the story, my progress, and my charity efforts. "Wow! What's NAMI?" he said. After giving him some examples about their programs and how I became drawn to them myself. "That's amazing!" he declared. "I just got out of the hospital. I was diagnosed bipolar; I tried to kill myself." His tone was so matter of fact. The concierge, who was the man's girlfriend, chimed in while checking me in, "I almost lost my baby."

"Do you take medicine?" asked the man. "This is my medicine," I replied, patting the seat of John Quick. He told me his name was Billy and asked if we could take a picture. I felt an overwhelming wave of pride and joy, like I was doing something right. I didn't hide my excitement at all, which only matched his. Billy told me all about how he would start exercising again tomorrow and his girlfriend gave me a heartwarming smile I'll never forget. She handed over my huge Domino's order and wished me a good night.

I know I was meant to meet Billy that night. In both of our lowest moments we crossed paths. Telling tales that support the essence of both our experiences collective and separate. He was a reminder to me why I was out here each day, suffering through the cold, rain, and 1000 other variables. For him, I was like a firefly on a long and quiet midnight walk. A brief glimpse of light incapsulated by darkness.

After meeting Billy I had a whole new appreciation for what I was doing again. I ate my nightly large Domino's pizza but with the new addition of a sandwich to wash down the Sprite. There was no time to relax though, with all the sand now permanently fused to my body and clothing, I needed to wash and ring out everything. It had been taking me longer and longer each night to shower and get ready for rest. Tonight, was especially hard with all the wet gear I had.

Drying out my stuff is a top priority; I hate when my shoes are still wet from the previous day. Getting rained on is one thing, but to deal with it the entire following day is a pain. When I finally took off my socks, I peeled off an entire layer of skin. The socks were thick and hard; I had never experienced anything like it. Washing those for only the second time in the trip was like ringing out aluminum foil. The crisp hard edges could have practically sliced me open. One good thing I had going for me was a small tub of shea butter that I had from Connecticut. The perfect cure. I lathered my feet with it until it dripped from the canyon size splits that ran down the center of both feet. Practically covered in lotions from head to toe, I passed out in sweet relief, butt naked on top of the bed.

BEAUFORT, SC TO JACKSONVILLE, FL

I WAS NOW STARTING to have some more... uh... stomach issues. My nighttime bathroom trips hadn't subsiding and were now becoming morning issues. While I was packing everything away, drying out my shoes with the room's hair dryer, I began shitting everywhere. I ran to the bathroom but kept dropping nugs all over the trail back to where it started. After I cleaned up my mess (because I'm not a fucking monster) I started packing everything quickly as I could. But I kept finding new droppings as I gathered my stuff. I stepped in glob after glob of loose stool only to have to hop on one foot to the bathroom to wash my feet. Once I thought it was taken care of, I'd step in another. This happened at least four times. I spent over half an hour stuck in this loop, cleaning the spots up on the floor. Extremely embarrassed, I left the remainder of my wallet for the hotel staff.

I needed to make a bathroom stop almost immediately after starting out. After more than a few minutes at a truck stop restroom, I emerged to a huge line a people with a smile on my face. It was less a self-satisfied smile and more an embarrassed, "I'm sorry" kind of smile. I knew this had to be fixed and fixed fast. I punched "pharmacy" into my GPS and chose the closest one. I went in and bought the first Pepto Bismol knockoff I could and ate a fistful. Instant relief.

I was now in palm tree country. They were everywhere and the spots to pee in the woods were a little diminished, the foliage ranging from no coverage between the spaced palms or such thick undergrowth that Bear Grills couldn't get through it.

The trees and the creatures who lived in them began to sing. They painted beautiful splashes of color and sound across this increasingly tropical landscape. There were now more and more white herons hanging out in ponds of all sizes. Smaller than their New England counterparts I was so used to seeing, they were no less beautiful. I watched their long legs protrude from the water to make their small frames appear as if they were hovering.

For me, one of the most revered parts of bike adventure is

animal watching. I get see a lot of animals I don't every day in the woods of New England. Once, in Montana approaching Glacier National Park, I was nearly trampled to death by wild horses. I've seen pelicans in North Dakota splash into a pond. Bald eagles dive bombing for their breakfast in Sand Point, Idaho. It is a true joy to see animals on the seat of your bicycle. You feel the rain with them and smell the same air. It's a deep sense of connection.

Out of nowhere, crossing a bridge, I rolled into Georgia and felt immense relief. A new state brings new beginnings, almost like a clean slate. Well, it was more a very grimy, dirty slate, but it was still a welcome one! Immediately, I passed into a protected wildlife habitat, one of their Audubon sanctuaries. I kept laughing at the "Bridge freezes before road" signs as I crossed them. There was certainly no ice around here; it was only 9 a.m. and the temperature was already soaring. Despite all the beauty, I was still peddling with a heavy heart after my interaction with Billy last night. Then I got a call from my dad, on his way to pick up my mom and drive her to work.

I told them all about meeting Billy and his girlfriend. How his eyes lit up and that I finally felt like I was making any sort of an impact on anyone. "You could've saved that guy's life," Dad said. I became completely washed away with emotion. Like someone standing on the ocean's edge, fighting the current, only to be pulled in by a whirlpool as ten-foot waves crash over them. My entire being was being tossed around in the sea of my own experience and struggles. I fell extremely quiet and I began to shudder. "I have to tell you guys something," I muttered in broken breaths to my parents. "I never wanted to tell you guys this, but I need to right now."

I told them about how my whole life I believed that I would inevitably kill myself. I never knew when this affirmation first began or how old I would be when it finally happened. It was this massive, planetary weight on my shoulders every second of every day, and I could almost watch it play out in my mind like a movie, this sad choose-your-own-adventure ending to my own biography. This was something I had held with me, even while training for this ride and advocating for others' mental health.

I always had this feeling like my existence burdened the lives of my family. I thought my birth was a grave mistake and I was a massive weight on them. My siblings would always tell me about how I was treated differently than them because I was the youngest. My next youngest sibling was my brother Jamie, still eight years my senior. My parents had split from their former partners out of some really bad situations. My mother used to get her ass kicked by her husband, and my father had a fucked-up wife too. There has always been an indescribably tense emotion that I never really understood from all my siblings. Even in times of love and comradery, they always had a chip on their shoulders toward me. I never knew how I could appease their disdain toward me. We do not choose to be born, but we are called upon. It is a terrible feeling to be cursed just for being born, I do not wish it upon anyone. Even as we have gotten older, the cycle remains the same. Something my dad once told me: "People don't change, they grow". I hope that these flowers will finally be able to grow above the weeds.

When I was researching charities, I discovered "Heads Up Guys", a subsidiary of NAMI. They are organized out of Canada with an emphasis on men's mental health. It was then that I felt like it could be otherwise. When reading testimonials from men of all different backgrounds, I came across someone who said, "I always thought my suicide was inevitable." That's when it hit me: I have control over this. That this was not some predetermined fate I had pulled the low card on. I can still recall riding away from work that day, just like any other day, feeling like my soul was cleansed. I had this dark and dirty feeling of guilt finally leave my body. It was the greatest gift I had ever received. All I had to do was allow it to happen.

My parents reacted how any great ones do, with love. They

never thought that their goofy, smiling, singing boy could carry this around with him. They made me feel worthy for one of the first times in my life. The constant, passive aggressive put downs from my brothers and sisters were being released from me.

I felt weightless again as I hung up the phone; I started to eat up some miles. My tenderized hands were starting to bother me more and more. I tried my best to get aero, lying flat and relaxed in the bars. The sun's rays intensified as I was pushing watts on this black, cracked asphalt. Everything was starting to get so hot that I had to keep drinking and drinking. It was not even mid-day and I felt like a cold-blooded pet, soaking up heat under a solar lamp. In an oven. In a house that was on fire. There was a method to my immense consumption though. I would drink both liters in my frame bag first and have to sit upright to grab my two bottles in the cages. One was an old water bottle, but the other was pretty exclusively a thirty-two-ounce Body Armor. They are basically coconut water-based Gatorades but without the high-fructose corn syrup. So, not only were they not thick in the heat, but the sugar didn't turn my stomach since the electrolytes were far more natural. I was guzzling the sweet, delicious nectar and spilling it all over myself at the same time. The road cracked and I bounced over its hazardous gaps, dribbling from my mouth to my toes like an infant. At this point, I was so irreparably dirty that it made no difference.

I was trying to switch up my diet to some "quieter", more easily available staples. Since I am mostly Irish, this was an obvious answer: potatoes. This was the perfect bang-bang lunch stop on a busy Georgia blacktop highway. I went to a gas station next to a Denny's, where my delectable root veggies were waiting, and filled up on Smartwater and two more Body Armors. I slugged one of those cane-sugary delights and went in on some hash browns and veggies. No lie, Denny's is actually a great spot for a vegan. The move (and you don't need to credit me on this) is to get the veggie scramble with no eggs. This way, it's just a mountain of veggies and potatoes. For extra calories and salt, I didn't take it easy on the ketchup. I was sitting in the first booth, helmet on, with a drink I brought in from a different store and the staff loved it. They went on and on to each other about how winter can't come fast enough so the tourists come back. What a difference to my snowy, hardwood New England upbringing.

I checked my email and Facebook to keep up on the messages as much as I could. At this point, several people had reached out to share their story with me and even more to try and help. My friend Lynn had struck again with her friends Mike and Connie. They lived in a town I was passing through and were eager to help. Connie was working part time as a swim instructor at their local YMCA while Mike was enjoying a full-time retirement. I was given their home phone number. Since he was available, Mike offered to meet me at this gas station just down the road from where they lived. It was time to put down some miles.

The hot air allowed my tires to cut like a knife through butter on the hot asphalt. Passing over bridges, I would pop out of saddle and add some more torque to the pedals, boosting me up and over the well-engineered water crossings lined by men fishing. Wind was favoring me for once and I was making great time. I finally felt prepared and ready for anything. It was an amazing feeling. I needed nothing but to lay down the power and meet my new friends. In the blink of an eye sixty more miles had disappeared beneath me.

I was able to get some actual food from a nearby Thai restaurant. Mike and Connie were so damn kind that they picked it up along with my food drop from the hotel I had originally booked at the start of the trip. This saved me a lot of money and even more time, since it meant I didn't have to head down a two-mile offshoot to get it myself or just leave it behind. I planned to meet him at a gas station on an intersection that would let me shoot south all the way from Jacksonville. If I could keep to my timetable, I planned to ride all of Georgia in less than a day.

I apparently had just missed Connie as I rolled into the gas station parking lot. She even called later to tell me that she saw me riding on her way to work the evening shift at the YMCA. Given the area and the complete lack of cyclists I had seen in days, I was most certainly whom she had seen.

These were the opportunities where my interactions far outweighed the time I'd save. I needed to starve the clock, but, most importantly, I needed to feed my heart. After this morning's emotional explosion of my raw and exposed heart to my parents, I was still feeling heart-wrenchingly empty. Mike was eager to see me. He was a quiet and stoic man who didn't seem like the sort of person to have a massive display of emotions, but I could see the light in his eyes. I thanked this guy who just drove to both edges of town for a total stranger and then waited for my stinky ass in the hot sun. I packed away my squirrely, stashed food and then went in on some rice and spring rolls. As I sat on the tailgate of his Ford Ranger, scarfing down these tasty noodles, I couldn't help but feel nostalgic. This was the same kind of truck that I learned to drive as a kid. I can still remember sitting on the tail gate at the shooting range with my dad as The Band played through the cassette deck. Mike is a retired engineer and Vietnam vet, a quiet man who is obviously very intelligent. While taking drags from his cigarettes, he told me all about how he and Connie got together. I listened as I ate, using my USPS box as a table. I thanked him multiple times, up, down, left, right, and he just said he was happy to help. His companionship, although short in duration, refilled my soul just like the Thai food filled my belly. Thanks, Mike and Connie. I owe you a nice dinner!

I gathered some liquids in the minimart. Unfortunately, because of my weak and decrepit hands, I dropped a bottle of Smartwater, which burst on the ground. Luckily, it was water and not something sticky. The shop owner was irritated but saw how genuinely sorry I was and didn't make me pay for it. Now I popped over to grab a 6-inch at the attached Subway. I asked them for the usual and crush a bag of chips over my sandwich. It was like presenting fire to a caveman. They were perplexed about the entire request, not processing that I couldn't really eat them while riding, at least not without spilling them all over the place and getting my grubby fingers all up in there. In effort just to get me out of there, they smushed the thing together and I stuffed it in my jersey. An odd exchange for everyone.

Back on the road, I was finally heading down Route 17, which ran the entirety of Georgia. It was a slightly down-pitched road that went through some small towns and big stretches of nowhere. The road was not very cleanly paved, and its vibrating surface was torturous, just miles and miles of the worst pavement of the whole adventure. More divots than a golf ball, it was vibrating through every possible contact point I had. Not only painful for my hands, feet, and saddle sores, but it also shook up my bladder. At this point, with my mastered quick bathroom stop, that wasn't really the issue. It was the thick brush lining the roadside where my worries lay. Their vines were like nets, just waiting to entangle a poor and hopeless cyclist and feed him to whatever giant ass snake was in there. No thanks.

The sun was finally starting to set, and I was getting close to my final and longest state: Florida. My mother called to tell me that the spot tracker was acting up again. The sun was just about gone at this point, and with no streetlights for miles, I had to swap out the batteries. I knew the state line was close and this stop really frustrated me. It took every fiber of my essence to stay calm. Immediately after, the neon beacon of a gas station emerged out of the early night darkness like an oasis out of thin air. It had everything a weary traveler could need. It wasn't much, but as far as gas stations in the middle of nowhere are concerned, it was certainly the nicest. I made my final stop to get more water and finish my remaining sandwich.

At this point, I was all sorts of excited. I thought, *I'm almost in Florida!* As I walked, my blinking, flashing, dancing lights and my bike's screaming rear hub caught the eye of everyone around. I had to buy some backup batteries for the spot tracker and get back on the road. Standing next to a mountain of Bud Light and polishing off my last 6-inch, I listened to the clerk, who seemed to end every sentence with "God bless." He said it as if he really meant that. He needed to get the last word in, not like he was controlling or assertive, but like he genuinely wanted to pass on love. Talking to the clerk was a man in some southern college football tee, cargo shorts, and a crooked smile charging his phone. Cargo shorts gave me the whole "Where ya goin'?" I told him of how I had left the border of Canada a week before. They looked at each other like they had just seen a Doug Flutie dropkick. "You're haulin' ass, boy," he exclaimed. The clerk nodded confidently in agreement.

I had a moment of clarity then. *I really am doing the damn thing*, I thought. Overcoming obstacle after obstacle to get to this point where I could actually break these challenges down one by one and figure it out. Small issues could have turned into major problems, but I had been managing them all, systematically working through these roadblocks (often literally) and staying cool, calm, and collected. I took off into the damp southern night, ready for another giant city crossing.

The stretch that crosses into Florida was just how you would picture. Little bayou bars with 4x4s playing country music and a big flat bridge across warm salty water. I had finally made it! I only had to get through Jacksonville. The moon illuminated the river as I crossed a near mile-long bridge to enter the Panhandle. I could see the city's skyline in the night just on the tip of my clawed fingers. After the state line, the excitement of being in Florida quickly passed as the difficulty of riding through the US's largest city set in. As the "Welcome to Jacksonville" sign appeared, so did waves of eyelid-shuddering exhaustion. It was time to find my way through this 875 square mile city at midnight, beginning at its crustiest part. There were dozens upon dozens of train tracks, so large I had to make sure to hit them sideways in my exhausted state. If you have ever crossed train tracks at high speeds before, you know the dangers of getting your wheel sucked in and being tossed off the bike if you're not careful. Sharp diagonal edges cut across multiple lanes of traffic as I bounced over the endless rail lines. My eyes were fluttering and no amount of Jolly Ranchers could cut it. I needed to stay as sharp as I could not to face the wrath of the magnetic pull of the steel beamed behemoths.

On my way into the city, it seemed like there was a four-to-one ratio of strip club to person, and all of them were busy. Thumping bass and neon colors flooded onto the dead street whose only inhabitants were a New Englander lost in the Deep South on his bicycle and the road workers who were beginning their nightly shifts. Their bulldozers moved slowly with giant signs and no particular direction other than forward. One of the benefits of bicycle travel is how police will let you pass in places where cars can't go. It seemed like the entire coalition of flaggers have passed word about me as I traveled down the coast.

Though I was nearly in the center of the city, I still had twelve miles to go. The massive span of Jacksonville is a tricky bit of geography at best, but most certainly far more overwhelming when traversing by bicycle. Just like any other major city though, its bustling city center quickly turned into sprawling suburbs. I called my friend Tim to try and stay awake. He's in the Air Force and is used to putting in the graveyard-shift. Grateful for you, brother!

I got to my hotel and said *au revoir* to my dear friend. I was staying at a motha-fucking Hilton! Even though I was paying the tab, it felt like a gift from the 10k Crew for that cold and wet night in New Jersey. I rolled in and saw a woman in her forties at the desk. Her beaming smile made me relax and enjoy some human interaction. She told me about how she loved to cycle despite her weak knees, how she was trying to get back into the swing of things. After I told her what I was doing, she said, "I always wanted to ride my bike across the country, but life got in the way and here I am." "There are always a million reasons why not to start," I told her. "Now is always the best time to take the first step."

Since I'd gotten into the habit of drinking soda again after years of avoiding them, those sugary bubbles were in high demand. I grabbed juices and sodas, candies, everything that would make my teeth rot. With my jersey pockets overflowing, I hobbled my way to the swanky elevator and up to my room where a Mediterranean feast was waiting for me.

My chores kept me up for at least another hour. Once again, I finished after midnight, and I still only managed to get five hours of sweat-drenched sleep, but the reset made me feel right.

JACKSONVILLE, FL TO VERO BEACH, FL

T HE NEXT MORNING was the kind of peaceful bliss where you should know shit's about to go down. I packed everything faster than normal so I could rush down to see the spread that the Hilton threw down for breakfast. There were half a dozen bottles of fresh pressed juice, an entire tree of bananas and an unreal oatmeal bar. It was my heaven. I piled two separate bowls filled to the brim with globs of peanut butter, walnuts, almonds, brown sugar, and golden raisins, only to pour a river of maple syrup over them. Every guest was smiling at one another, even at the stinky cyclist. I sat down at a long table in the center of the room, facing a wall of windows. As I stuffed my stomach to capacity, I saw the weather reports. They predicted heavy storms coming off the ocean to smash central Florida, exactly where I was heading. Chugging fresh tropical juice to wash down all the nutrients I so badly needed, I couldn't even imagine today being anything less than this serene moment of time. Florida showers, right?

After checking out, I realized I had forgotten to fill up my water, so I made a quick stop at a gas station just down the road. Grabbing as much Smartwater as I could, I checked out quickly to get on the road. Without even thinking, I bought an extra bottle. As I looked up, a nurse on her way to her morning shift walked in. I offered her the bottle, which she accepted with an ear-to-ear grin. It seemed a small gesture but felt good to help someone who selflessly aids others day after day with no thanks in return.

I was now getting close to the beginning of the A1A, Florida's scenic State Road that rides the coast all the way to Miami. It was morning rush hour, and the road was packed with impatient commuters. I had to make a decision about my route and set the tone for the day. I knew that storm was coming. I had been outside for a week now and was in tune with the weather, even a place I was unfamiliar with like Florida. Staying off the coast made the most sense despite the busy roads and drab highway. I made the choice to make a big push on Route 1, A1A's less good-looking older brother. What I would sacrifice in visual distractions would be made up for in the most precious resource of all: time.

It was time for another call from Jon, Joe, and Courtney at WPOR. I was excited. They had brought a whole new element to the trip. They were bringing more awareness to my cause and personally shining light on me while I gave myself fully to the ride. There was a live action kind of feel between their reporting and my tracker. Jon caught word that I had no sponsors and had completely self-funded this trip to raise money for NAMI. This morning he made sure everyone knew this and plugged my efforts. I never wanted to ask anyone for money for this. After the accident, I really went under on this trip. Everything from months of planning was gone. I'd purchased a bike, tickets, accommodations; everything had been sorted out, and it had all been thrown away. On the phone with the station thousands of miles away, Jon's mention of it made me feel like a stoic adventurer, set out in an expedition.

These moments in life are when you realize it's more than a cacophony of insane thoughts moshing in your brain. When dots finally link up on a cardboard wall you have been shaping for over a year. I was creating meaning for the ever important "why". A map of tireless strings connecting the hardworking tacks to support a better world around us. In any shape or form, this is always a life worth living. Here I was, some random dude just trying his best to help people around me. Without the succession of awful things screaming in your face, you can be blindly smashing through obstacles and forget to open your point of view. Without the clouds, you won't appreciate the sun.

As the day passed, hours of burning rubber on a hot Florida highway was getting old. I was making good time moving with the metal behemoths around me, but I needed proper scenery. I eventually jumped on A1A, somewhere by the town of Palm Coast. This put the ocean almost within arm's reach, and I marveled at its dangerous beauty, watching its currents churn as dark cloud built and swirled above. I knew I was in for something soon. On the bright side, due to the imminent rain, a strong tailwind was burning me along. Eating up the miles, easily coasting along 18-20 mph, I was making some serious time. It felt like I was being pushed endlessly forward on a swing.

Soon I began seeing other bikes. Passing cyclists for the first time in what felt like months was jarring. They were flying into the wind in a tight line like birds before a storm. Only a couple days away from the finish, I stopped to do some much needed maintenance. A picturesque bike shop off A1A let me come in just before they opened. I wiped away a pound of grime from my jockey wheels and chain, using a blue shop towel they gave me. The cassette was already rounding off and the chain had stretched substantially. It looked like a slack Nerd's Rope that had been seriously used and abused by shark teeth the past week. I used the rest of my chain lube and pumped my tires up for the first time since D.C. Those two small things make the biggest differences in the performance of both the bike and your mind. After removing the South Carolina mud caked on my drive train, I had a fresh dose of confidence in my trusty steed and felt lighter. I was quick. I wanted to take advantage of the monster tailwind that was still cooking. Plus, at any minute, with the massive front moving in, I knew it was about to change.

The wind picked up as if land and sea banded together. Palm trees began to bend easier than a #2 pencil, while sea walls hopelessly deflected massive ocean waves crashing down like thunder. I felt the first couple drops and knew I was in for more than a passing mid-day Florida shower. "Quick in, quick out" was not in the forecast today. Just as I pulled over to put on my rain clothes, I got a call from Mary, in D.C. She told me she created a press package for me and sent it to some media outlets in the Keys. Unbelievable! In her quick thinking, she put together an amazing writeup on me. There were a couple groups who immediately responded, and she even got me an interview with US1 radio, right on the island. The only thing was, I had to make it there in time to land the interview. I had to get moving.

As the screaming sidewinds off the Atlantic slid me up and across a long bridge, multi-million-dollar mansions immediately gave way to fleets of RVs. They were parked and organized on concrete slabs overlooking the ocean, much like how I imagined my grandparents used to park theirs. Every year, they would drive their old RV all the way down Route 1 from North Central Massachusetts. Their path was similar to the one I'd taken to this very point and I knew I was getting close to where they used to stay. My grandmother passed a little before I rode cross country and was my inspiration to raise money for St Jude's. Being pale Irish folk, skin cancer is common in our family and it took her life. My grandfather always follows along during my big trips and told me of the oceanic beauty of this part of Florida.

But that beauty was difficult to see at the moment. The rain was now ripping even harder. Like a sidearm pitcher, water was coming in sideways, fast and unpredictable. Anywhere that wasn't level flooded within minutes. Roads were already blocked off (probably from the storm that had hit me two days ago) and my tailwind was now a soul crushing headwind. I was trying to avoid doing bike math and laid down on my aero bars, trying to relax. I began to feel wet all across my back. Just as I reached back I realized that the wind was hitting so hard off the side of ocean that it was blowing straight through my jacket. First it was jarring and slightly worrisome, but it wasn't as cold as Connecticut, and I knew my body heat would dry it if I zipped back up.

Pushing along, just as I started to feel sorry for myself, I saw my first touring cyclist since the morning of day two. He was on the sidewalk, trying to avoid the constant swerve into the road, away from the puddles. I remember the long days of pushing a steel touring bike with all those bags into the headwinds for hours. It was like running parachute drills, except no one would ever take the damn parachute off. I gained on him quickly and shouted out to him. His name was Oscar, a recent departure from the military and in between school. He was riding across the country to Key West of all places. After trading a few stories, I told him to tuck in behind me. To earn the record, I couldn't have anyone in front—that was technically drafting—but he could. I made sure to soak up the brunt of Mother Nature's anger as he fell in tight behind me. A detour sign forced us off the ocean highway into nearby neighborhoods. Popping one street over got us out of the wind momentarily.

If you've ever been in a screaming headwind while holding a conversation, you know that it's like talking to a mirror. He asked what I was doing, about my goals and my story. I told him that I started on the border just over a week prior, pushing 200-220 a day while raising money for the record to raise money for NAMI. I was feeling wide open at this point. Sharing a hard experience with a person will do that to you. I went into my past, how I used to be angry and how cycling had turned my life around. This intrigued him, and he asked a bunch of leading questions. This seemed like an opportunity to share some knowledge that had been given to me. I spoke about my meditation practice and plant-powered ideologies. I said that I truly believed those two things can turn your life around, that they had for me. When I told him how hard I had worked to get to this point and I finally was figuring stuff out, I realized that I finally believed the words as they left me. I had trained like a madman to get here and faced so much adversity already. I knew that nothing was going to stop me. Whether I finished smiling or scowling, I was going to fucking do it.

I believe that it is your duty to pass on knowledge. It should be free, but knowledge is power and that is most likely why we are restricted by pay walls and forced responsibilities. It is your responsibility to share that power with those around us. Nothing is more powerful than a person at a crossroads given the tools to succeed. The weight of the decision can feel like the shoulders of giants supporting everyone around you. You must use these shared powers in times of stress and hardship. The decision to put the best foot forward every time is what creates success in any shape or form. The metaphorical, and in my case literal, hours of darkness are what people don't see. Your choice to do, or not do, will bring you to the ultimate.

We enjoyed each other's company while we traded road stories. When you're alone, traveling for a long period of time, it becomes the new normal: just you, your bike and the endless expanse of your mind. Oscar's bike had the mount for a handlebar bag, but he had left it somewhere out west. By the time he had realized, it was way too far to turn around. I loved the beauty of this story. How unaffected he was, almost like he did it on purpose. I guess we need a lot less than we really think. Smoking pot with mountain dwellers in Colorado, passing herds of wild buffalo in Yellowstone, he was having a great trip. Enjoying his time and soaking it all in, I was happy to see someone living their dreams.

We stopped to grab some food and enjoy the spoils of the road. I knew that I had a solid day ahead and needed some grub. Meanwhile, he had a WarmShowers host just ahead in Daytona Beach. We smashed Subway sandwiches and Oreos in a road-side gas station. I re-upped on snacks and water even though

I could just open my mouth for a drink. We pushed on ahead and he tucked right in behind me again as the last twelve miles disappeared from under us. Just as we got into the tourist trap that is Daytona Beach, he told me, "That's the fastest I've gone on the entire trip." For me, I was just excited to have someone in a similar headspace. We parted ways, exchanged contacts, and wished each other luck. Thanks for the vibes, brother!

As A1A disappeared and turned back into US-1, the rain changed from wet to monsoon in the blink of an eye. Visibility dropped to nearly zero and the road was swallowed by the torrential downpour. The combination of tall buildings and bad weather sent my spot tracker into weather-related woes. I had to fix it as fast as possible. I came to an accidental screeching halt under an awning occupied by families on vacation. They seemed to have a mixture of interest and fear as my disc brakes squealed and I pulled up next to them to fidget with my tracker.

The rain fell so hard and my glasses were so wet that I could almost see better without them. The roads turned to rivers and all my stuff became soaked almost immediately. My waterproof bags would've been very highly rated as an off-grid water collection system right now. They were pooling up anywhere my zippers weren't shut tight. My phone wasn't charging, and my iPod stopped working. I forced myself to remain calm; I needed to figure something out fast to save my emergency contact and GPS device. In a turn of good fortune, I found a surprisingly nice gas station, smack in the middle of Nowhere, Florida. There were no town centers for miles and the people here were like characters out of a television show, a Cheer's establishment where everyone knew your name, except mine of course. I watched them buy their afternoon tall boys of Budweiser cocktails and tins of dip as I dripped hopelessly on their floor. Having the good fortune to find an Xlerator hand dryer in the bathroom, I began the process of drying my gear. It was a layered moment of priorities, as my dedicated electronics bag had completely filled with water. I needed to dry out my phone first. My iPod only needed a quick blast of air to light up again. Somehow my battery pack was mostly dry from the plastic bag that held it and the cables. After some troubleshooting, the cable to the pack was broken, not the unit itself. My sense of relief soared, even if for a moment. I soaked up the water in the bag with fistfuls of napkins. The cashier had been watching the whole ordeal and offered plastic baggies to wrap my stuff in. The unplanned stop was unwelcome, but losing everything would have been worse.

As soon as I left the station, the rain stopped for a moment. I was grateful; I had been drenched for hours and couldn't handle another trench foot night like I had in Beaufort. Afternoon rush hour was starting to begin again, and the road grew busier by the moment. Since I didn't allocate for the stop, I lost the time I gained earlier from the tailwind. Instead of pulling over, I decided to take off my shoe covers and socks while riding so I could let my feet dry. Though kind of scary in traffic, it was exciting to try a little trick while riding. At this point, I could do your taxes without stopping. I began to carefully peel away the damp, sandy layers from my wrinkly feet. If I wasn't careful, I'd easily just rip the bike off in the wrong direction and dump it. I slipped the shoe covers onto my handlebars so they could dry. As their neon-yellow nylon bodies fluttered in the wind, I peeled my socks off and left them at the tips of the bars to let my pruned digits breathe. I felt like I had just given birth to these soaking wet, screaming foot babies. They were tender, sitting on top of my shoes while I was peddling, getting smooshed into the bare Velcro and hard plastic boa dial with its dancing wire. With the only damage being a brief pause to find my dropped sock about fifteen feet behind me, it felt like it was one of the most successful problems I solved the whole trip.

Adventure demands you to figure out problems without hesitation. Depending on the medium, a small misstep or minor miscalculation could mean damaged equipment, injury, or even death. Long distance cycling requires you to stay attentive and cool. Burning in anger will waste energy that will cut your day short or cause you to make brash decisions. Losing your attention could mean falling asleep while riding or drifting off into traffic, both fatal mistakes from small lapses in judgement. I might not have had the potential to ice axe my belay line, but cycling is a numbers game. I was playing to win with the big boys, and I was playing all the cards on the table.

Still barefoot, I continued to peddle for a few more hours until the sun started getting low and I wanted to grab another 6-inch for the road. I kept scrolling through Google Maps looking for that coveted truck stop gold when I remembered my iPhone cable was still broken. My phone was dying, and it was my primary navigation at this point. There was no wasting time digging through my bags just to repack it I thought. Then in my semi-delirious state, I saw a CVS ahead.

I walked into the CVS looking like the homeless person I was. Rain clothes hanging off my body: jacket and jersey unzipped below my belly button, pants rolled up into shorts, and barefoot. This was the turning point of becoming fully feral. I lost all connection to any fragment of societal rules or acceptance. I'd been on the road, pushing both my mind and body to a state I never had before, a kind of self-propelled traveler's flow state. There was no reason to adhere to signs of minor inconvenience. These were hall monitor restrictions put on those who aren't trying to walk blindly through life. I was on a mission and these were small obstacles trying to fight my fate.

Like a zombie possessed to eat brains, my tunnel vision mindlessly propelled me to fix my next problem. I walked in and saw the first cashier, a young woman, around my age with dyed red hair and a nose ring. We locked eyes and I smiled to diffuse her obvious unrest with my disheveled appearance. This usually gets me out of most situations, but I was way off the deep end here. She ducked her head and did the whole "I can't see you" hand over her eyes as she power walked past me. I found a carousel of overpriced electronics by the register and grabbed a cord. There were three ladies in line, one who looked like she would've shot me right there if she had been able. "Could I please cut you in line?" I pleaded with my fellow drugstore consumers. Just as the unrest tipped the scales, a middle-aged woman who had seen a thing or two came over. She opened a register just for me. The pop-punk cashier whispered to her not quietly enough, "He doesn't have any shoes on!" She gave her a look that said she was aware but just wanted to get me the hell out of the store. I made my purchase and walked outside back to the bike.

Just as I opened the package with my Silly Putty hands, I

realized that I had bought the wrong cord. I was pissed, the last bits of my patience disappearing with my mistake. I whipped the overpriced cable into the trash like the last pitch of the World Series and stomped back inside to repeat the whole process. Carousel. Charger. Back to the same cashier. Our conversation was like a teenage boy and his disappointed mother. "What happened?" she asked me with care. "I bought the wrong cord," I replied monotone and frustrated. "Well, where is it?" Embarrassed that I had not only wasted money, but time and resources, I told her the truth. She sighed and I paid for a new one, ferociously clawing at the box. "Let me just help you," she said as she grabbed the box from my bear paws and opened it. I scampered away frustrated. I re-organized my top tube bag and got back on the road. A couple minutes later, I began hysterically laughing as I descended into madness.

The sun had now set upon the endless highway and I was back on the large shoulder of Route 1. Its sandy edges were my home now, and all I could do was keep moving forward. Ever so carefully, I took my jacket off while I was riding and tied it around my waist. My arms kept getting stuck, but I had to keep both hands on the jacket to prevent it from getting sucked into my rear wheel. By no means was this the right way to go about it, but in my delirious state of existence, the consequences were irrelevant. I called my dad and he told me about his adventures as a kid and the time he got in a car wreck while driving a bread truck. The couple who caused the crash both died, and he was left with only scrapes and bruises from the seat belt. In my sleep-deprived, hungry state his words trickled into my ears like a roll of film flowing through a projector. I could feel the damp air as they crashed into the tree and the flames that I imagined engulfing their automobile. It was somehow an oddly comforting moment of relief.

Never forget the endless wisdom of your elders. Even if you live a life rich of experience, they have experienced more than you. Take notes, and respect. Over the course of time, we encounter exponentially fresh experiences. One could only live their life and come across certain happenings. My father's story reminded me of how little I really know. Even with societal norm cast aside in my feral state, I was again grounded with perspective.

I was hungry and still needed to grab some food. I passed through a small town, the last before the big gap to Vero Beach, where I would stop for the night. On the last intersection of town there was a Subway and a convenience store. Even though I had snacks, I wanted something that would occupy some space in my stomach, rather than just giving me calories. I rolled across the double lanes to the Subway. "If there is a big line or anything that will waste my time, I'm getting out of there," I said out loud. Inside I found a guy had ordered half a dozen sandwiches and was arguing with the man making them. The disgruntled customer screaming, "I said no lettuce!" might as well have been Gandalf with his staff shouting, "You shall not pass!" I swiftly went to the convenience store, defeated and hungry.

Sinking even lower than before, I knew I had to get back on the road. I was exhausted from the rain and all the problem solving it required. In any way, shape, or form, I needed a boost. Early on, I had tried a 2 a.m. coffee whose only gift to me was warmth. Deep in the South, I didn't need any more warmth and certainly no more wet. I grabbed a serving of my Athletic Greens, a vitamin drink mix that had been powering me the entire trip. *For those who live a stressful lifestyle or are very active, take 2 servings*, it read in bold contrasting writing on the label. Perfect! I was both of those. I asked the cashier if I could grab a cup from the stack beside her. This hole-in-the-wall shop sold freshly roasted peanuts in Nalgene-sized paper cups, which I was only charged a quarter for. I poured just enough liquid into the green, sea algae mixture to make it into something that resembled a liquid. I shot the concoction back and then went to their back alley to pee since their restroom was closed.

Up to this point, I had been taking these green vitamin mixes every single morning. The only other time I had taken athletic greens twice in a day was just before my 3-a.m. push out of Maine into Massachusetts. This time was completely different. I felt like Bruce Banner, turning into the Hulk for the first time. All of a sudden my senses were blown wide open; every sound, every light was intensified. I could smell colors and see sounds as my skin began to crawl. The Jolly Ranchers were spinning like a washing machine out of control in my mouth. They chattered across my teeth and bounced off my tongue almost violently as I rode away from that god-forsaken town. The sensory overload made the sugary blocks feel like I had someone's teeth moving around in my mouth. "I have teeth in my mouth!" I yelled manically on the side of the dark highway. My heart was racing. My temperature soared like I had the flu. I broke out into a feverish sweat and ripped over to the side of the road, suddenly overcome with the urge to rip off my rain gear. Shaking my head like I was on a meth binge screaming, "No one better fuck with me right now! I will rip out your throat and eat it!" to the crowd of zero people around. Tearing off my rain gear felt like a relief, but my bath salts freak out continued. I couldn't vent enough heat from my elevated state. The flames inside me bellowed up from my heart to my skull. Evacuating heat from my helmeted forehead, I loosened it all the way and tilted it back. My exposed cranium felt the humid night air wrestle with the demons that wanted to escape me.

Amidst my freak out I at least remembered to ask Olyvia how her packing was going. I called her as she was at our apartment with her three sisters and their mom, getting ready to fly to Miami the following morning. The state of my being was dark and completely un-empathetic. She was stressed about her trip and forgetting something. I couldn't imagine how she could be anything but content and filled with love in our cozy apartment with her family beside her. I snarled something stupid and insensitive over the phone to her and immediately felt awful about it. No one, especially her, deserved to take any of the raging heat inside me. Desperate for love and forgiveness, I apologized profusely to her and wished her a safe flight in the early morning.

We are often quick to snap at the ones we love and are comforted by. Thinking that they will see through our debilitated state and the truth of being frosted with ourselves or situations. There was no reason to get mad at my situation and especially at my dear, sweet Olyvia who loves me so much. Hell, she was going to fly to Miami in the morning and come be my support crew on the final day. Hopefully, the support of food, water, and really just another set of eyes would propel me forward. This wasn't even our original plan either. She was just going to meet me for the finish and now had an extra responsibility.

No matter how close to home or how far you've been riding, knowing that you are within striking distance of the end plays with your mind. Close enough that no snacks are needed but far enough that deep suffering can begin from nothing. This is routinely the hardest part of every ride. I was about an hour and a half from my hotel and couldn't keep myself from stopping for trivial things. Suddenly, I was getting wet for the 100th time of the day and couldn't imagine being without rain clothes for a second, even with the warm tropical night air. I passed another small RV park on the edge of the ocean with a long dirt driveway. I paused and leaned my bike against a large aluminum mailbox to make it easier to grab my rain gear. I forged through the sandy soil and sharp crab grass and slipped my pants back on. I had taken only two steps when my ankles began to sting and itch uncontrollably. A deep primal scream emerged from me as a burning sensation radiated from the nerves around my ankles and spread through my body. I began screaming and rolling around the edge of the highway. I tore my rain pants off and found they were filled with fire ants. They were gnawing at my skin, chewing away at my flesh, softened from the day of sopping, wet rain. I began frantically shaking my pants around like I was possessed. Like a maniac, I strapped them down to the top of my seat pack and rode away like I could outride the pain. The burning continued as I slapped the ants away. Eventually, I sprayed half a bottle of water across myself to get the bastards off me. I guess this brings a whole new perspective on ants in your pants!

Still an hour away from my hotel, I kept forging on, my only thoughts about just lying down on the side of the road, letting those devil ants feast on my body. Picking away chunks of flesh as I went into anaphylactic shock. Picturing the sand creeping into every crevice and letting Mother Nature bury me beneath the tides. If I stayed much longer, I surely would've succumbed the poison shock of the fire ants. With the gleaming red damage already done to my ankles, I knew that it wouldn't have taken too much longer.

To stay awake, I began just making noise. Shouting incoherent sounds and noises. Flapping my lips like a chimpanzee and shaking my head like a wet dog, emerging from a lake. There wasn't a car in sight, but even if there had been a tour bus filled with families on vacation, it wouldn't have mattered. I was a wild man, mid-battle, who wasn't going to let anyone or anything stop him from his goal. However, even in my determination, I was still struggling to remain awake.

I called the only person I knew was up right now, my sister Sarah. Recent mother of two, doctor of chiropractic medicine, and fellow insomniac, she picked up just before midnight. After telling her of the day's turmoil, she began laughing hysterically like I had earlier. Right away, I realized how ridiculous and hilarious everything was. Misery loves company, but, truly, no one wants more pain. The essence of the midnight air and laughter with my sister filled my heart with joy once again. She was the only one of my siblings that took sustained time with me. My siblings were so much older than me, but I never understood why they didn't make time for me until I had a life of my own. I think Sarah was different because of an accidental sixteen-mile hike in the Adirondacks when I was thirteen. We went off trail to find a World War II bomber plane that had crashed into the side of the mountain where we were hiking and got horrendously lost looking for it. We laughed at the chaos of everything, lost and hungry. Her fresh perspective of my perceived "suffering" brought light to my dark situation.

Out of nowhere, I was at Vero Beach. Like a stunt driver, I screeched into the Econo Lodge parking lot and went inside to check in. In an odd coincidence, the overnight receptionist who had the luck of hosting this disgusting hobo with an expensive bike was also from Massachusetts and had moved down to Florida to change her life. I have always admired that characteristic in people.

My nightly chores were going to be a bit longer tonight with the whole ants in the pants ordeal. Though I was attacked by their entire community, I still hated to kill even insects. Ever since I went vegan, I began to witness senseless violence in our everyday lives. What seems like an insignificant pest is a life, even if it is a pain in the ass. Failing to rinse all hundreds of them off my inside out rain pants, I hand no choice but to go in to squish them all one by one. I ate my weight in noodles, soup, and bread soaked in a lake of olive oil. I ate my last CBD gummy, used the end of my salve, and finally shut my eyes.

VERO BEACH, FL TO FLORIDA CITY, FL

I AWOKE FEELING LIKE I had sprouted fur and fangs under a full moon. Yesterday's series of ordeals had turned me fully feral. There was no going back now. There was a call of the wild that would resist and snarl at any obstacle. I was laser focused and nothing would stop me.

I went to grab the continental breakfast that I'd been surviving on. The way I was looking at it, it was taking money off the hotel since I was covering a full meal. The spread was typical this morning, but the concierge was a stellar guy. An Indian man in his late thirties, he was talking politics with his mechanic while drinking coffee. As I made half a loaf of toast and crushed an apple, I kept chuckling at his tenacity. He turned to me and told me he had heard of me before. This man was apparently the manager and took great care of his little Econo Lodge in Vero Beach. He asked legitimate questions that most people don't normally ask: Is someone from Guinness going to meet you there? How many news outlets are covering this? Are you getting anything from this? I told him how Guinness charges folks nearly a grand to have someone at the end of the attempt, that no one had picked up the story, and how *giving back* was what I was getting from it.

This turned his fire up from trashcan to a dozen dry Christmas trees. "Are you kidding me, man?" he shouted. "More people need to know about you, man. This is fucking amazing. You are the real deal, man!"

I chuckled. "I'm just a dude riding his bike, brother."

"No," he was adamant, "You don't realize how amazing this is. You're out here risking your life, spending your money to help other people. The world *needs* to know this story, man." He turned to his mechanic and asked, "Can you fucking believe this, man? He wants nothing, *nothing*!" I felt a surge of gratitude for this new figure. It was if he had watched me battle down the coast, fighting for those who can't. I felt appreciated and noticed for the first time of the whole trip.

The thing is, I'm not looking for appreciation; I absolutely love every second of a wild adventure. But the point is that this spiritual journey is supposed to represent something for other people. A hard-fought battle to work through complicated and complex emotions that I've suppressed, unknowingly, for years. If people did small and considerate actions more often, the world would be such a better place. If you are constantly in pursuit of the right moral action, with a willingness to learn and adapt to new knowledge, you can never be wrong. Admitting your mistakes and growing from them, consciously and caringly. People often tell me, "Well, people don't really live like that."

But someone has to.

As I checked out, the man told me all about his son, who puts on fun runs to raise money for ALS. This man was so proud of his son, and I believe he saw him in me. We thanked each other in our goodbye, and he wished me good faith. My heart hadn't felt this full during this journey, where each day felt like a lifetime.

I was now foaming at the mouth. Ready to fight the wind and the rain. To burn so hot that the water would evaporate like a stove top. "My feet are not getting wet today," I snarled to my adventure mascot Mr. Crabman, who had seen more water in the past week than a real crab would in his whole life. It was a typical Florida morning, rain on one side of the street and bone dry on the other. It was already hot, but I was by no means going to get road spray in my shoes and shorts. It was an hour-long off-and-on battle with my rain gear amongst the rush hour traffic along Route 1.

As the hours passed it got a lot hotter and, though rain was in the forecast, the sky was bright blue from horizon to horizon. "We might be lucky today, Mr. Crabman," I said to my sewn-in smiling counterpart. Though a pale Irishman, heat doesn't break me down like other people. I made sure to stay up on the sunscreen, reflecting the rays in the whole spectrum, but there are also little tricks you can do to keep from cooking internally. I like to rotate my drinking water. My multiple vessels would warm at different times, which meant I could drink them in that order before they got too hot. I'd start with my exposed bottle and move to my bladder in the frame bag. I would also hold ice to the roof of my mouth until it melted and put sopping wet paper towels in my helmet. The slow drip down the back of my neck was practically an aphrodisiac. Depending on how hot it was (just before 11 a.m. it was already over ninety and the forecast showed it was going to steadily climb) the towel would dry and then I'd use it to wipe something gross, which is easy to find, before tossing it. The last trick was to make sure to use indoor bathrooms. They offered brief cooling breaks where I'd chug water and re-stock on fluids. It wasn't so much that I needed to pee—I was sweating so god damn much—my body really just needed more water. At this point I was on a strict bourgie diet of Smartwater and CORE coconut water drinks to make sure all my electrolytes were not being missed.

I left the last town's gas station just before hitting a long nature reserve. It felt like a desert. Sand dunes stretched as far as the eye could see with only scattered, small vegetation on the ground. It was a complete and fully immersive hot-weather experience. The heat kept rising and now there was absolutely no shade or civilization for miles in either direction. Barely 11 a.m. and the pavement was already dancing on the horizon. The steaming heat waves drew me in like sirens on a dangerous, battered coastline. There was no avoiding the oven that I had thrown myself into.

Too hot even to listen to a podcast, I had just removed my earbuds when Olyvia called. She told me she landed safely and was clearly excited from her trip. I could hear it in her voice; she was bubbling from the flight and being in a brand-new environment. This was fun and exciting for her, and I tried not to be too brash. We have silly arguments over her misinterpreting my directness when I'm in a feral state. It's my own fault that I'm not communicating better. Sometimes words take too much away from your mental capacity when all you really need is to *do*. We worked out the plan for the day and what we needed. It was going to be great that I would actually have someone to look out for me and help me, hopefully bringing me in before midnight tonight. It would be hours before I'd see her, but we would end up meeting in a beautiful spot.

As I left the nature preserve, WPOR called me for another interview. I told them the ants in the pants story and laughed with them. Though I would have put up a good fistfight against a gorilla right now, I was trying not to take myself too seriously. After all, I am just a dude on his bike. They asked me what "comfort items" I took along. I chuckled before realizing they were serious and said simply, "A second pair of underwear." I fell victim to their infectious laughs and kindhearted jostling. The playful tones gave me bubblings of some childlike fun as I hopped a curb at the bottom of a long driveway.

Civilization soon appeared like a mirage after my desert dwellings. I bombed down a massive bridge and a sign for A1A appeared. I had been avoiding it to stay dry because I knew the traffic and sun would dry out Route 1 first. Switching to A1A was an instant gratification decision. I was gifted shade, a gentle breeze, and a view of the ocean. The sweet salty air kissed my skin while I watched surfers stroll along the white sand. It looked like puréed coconut. Jeep Wranglers with surfboards poking out of the back lined the streets. I was finally in coastal Florida and felt renewed to see what this new environment had to offer.

This was immeasurably more affluent than every other part of Florida I had seen so far. RV parks were replaced with high-rise hotels. For every tricked-out Wrangler, there were two sets of boat shoes and coral-colored shorts. I was rolling pretty quick, passing edible restaurants that had actual nutrients. These were godsends after endless days of typing "vegan" into Google Maps and getting Subway as my only option. Now, it was almost hard to make a decision, but once Meraki Juice Kitchen popped on my radar and I saw that they had a smoothie called "Blue Dream", this was a no brainer.

Crowds were so dense that there was nowhere for me to use the bathroom discretely. I knew I could make my next stop without more water, but I couldn't wait to find a toilet. I slipped into a small restaurant that was packed to the gills, ignoring the awkward stares from waitresses and customers who very clearly knew I would not be eating there. After bumping and brushing against everyone in my path, I smelled more like fried food than weeklong stank.

Once I finally arrived at the Meraki Juice Kitchen, it was clear that my veracious focus combined with my Northeast speed put me on a different frequency than this kicked back smoothie spot. There were two dudes working behind the counter. Both had Vans and mid-calves on, floating from station to station while underground hip hop boomed and bapped in the background. This was a place I could sit and write a for a while. I quickly snapped out of the vibes and ordered a sprout and avocado sandwich on Ezekiel bread, a fatty carb-filled gift from god. My cells screamed in enjoyment and my stomach purred like an idling Ferrari. This was that premium gas that I needed. I was about to get one hell of a smoothie for the road too.

You always hear about the awful food that explorers survived on. Pemmican and other gross shit like that. I met a guy who just rode a touring motorcycle all around Alaska and he gave me a stick of some meat. To this day I still don't know what it was. Maybe bull testicles for all I was concerned. It was quickly hidden amongst my friend's belongings later that day. That kind of mentality has been adopted by the whole ultra-scene. I mean I totally get all the salty, fatty cravings when you are low on calories and have been burning diesel like an 18-wheeler for literal weeks, but there is always a better solution to these needs. The sprouts and loaded avocado had all the healthy fats my body needed but that I had been stuffing with chips and oil from Subway. This sandwich was more than just calories, it was actual nutrition. Now, instead of some Oreos to top off my glycogen, I was about to get a berry-loaded smoothie with hemp protein and spirulina powder. Most importantly, this meal meant no emergency bathroom stops, so I'd actually get to use these calories for something productive.

I left the surf dudes to get back on the road. There was less than an hour between me and my loving wife. Someone to watch my six and to experience this with. She had just hit the grocery store for us to cover the next two days, and I would get to offload some of my equipment when I saw her. I just had to traverse some serious Florida stop-and-go traffic.

I could see West Palm Beach now in all its iconic Florida sunshine. Olyvia and I would meet on a neighborhood side street where all the houses looked like they might have been owned by Pablo Escobar. I took a wide corner and saw the white Nissan she had rented from the airport. Her huge nervous smile quickly turned into a look of awe. We had spoken on the phone constantly, but other than my update videos on Facebook, she hadn't seen me at all. The first thing she said to me was, "You are so dirty!" Oddly, it put me at ease. She could see the stains on my jersey and the dirt strewn all over my body. Not to mention a knot the size of a softball in my hair. There was something about surprising someone who knew more than anyone else about the trip that made me feel even more like a wild animal.

Besides being reunited with my better half and seeing some-one I knew, I was excited to ditch some junk. It wasn't much, but things like getting my plastic bag wallet and sunscreen out of my jersey pocket really helped me keep cool. After a couple swigs from the kombucha she brought and a quick kiss, off I went down the A1A. I couldn't fall into her soft, warm embrace yet; I was too close to fuck things up now.

West Palm Beach is the kind of place you see in movies. Lawns manicured like golf courses, deco mansions with a Tesla in every driveway. It was one of the parts of the trip I was most excited about. I was making great time with the flat terrain and gentle ocean breeze, the exact opposite of yesterday. There were dark clouds ahead, which of course played with the PTSD of the twenty-four prior, but I kept my head down. I mean, I had to, there were lizards everywhere! Scurrying across the road at the last minute just like the squirrels of New England but with way funnier butts. Their tails waved and danced as they pushed their way to safety underneath the coconut trees, whose tasty, fatty, delicious fruit I had to dodge like shells in Mario Kart.

Despite the traffic, I was actually cranking along the A1A. A work van and I came up to a red light at the same time. He was blasting The Mighty Mighty Bosstones, Boston legends, onto the street. I turned over to him and started shouting the lyrics to get his attention. I caught his attention and we had one of those great human experiences. Two strangers wrapped in a story of coincidences. He wished me luck and rocked out into the mid-day heat nearly causing an accident. You just can't fight the rock!

Olyvia was actually way behind me at this point. It was now rush hour traffic and we were on a beach road with tons of stoplights and even more construction. We had planned to meet at this vegan cafe just outside Miami called The Green Bar & Kitchen. My wheels were cranking along on the hot Florida asphalt and I was on pace to make it there before her, so she called ahead to order a veggie burger with fries for me. The place was like entering a different universe. The air was lighter, and everyone was so kind. To compliment my veggie burger and fries, I bought a beet juice and a face-sized brownie. Olyvia made great timing after the construction and walked through the doors looking like a goddess. At this point, I was so accustomed to my speed eating, my quick in-and-out ways that I didn't think about how I looked at all. Still wearing my helmet, dripping sweat and sunscreen, inhaling a burger with beet juice dripping from my mustache. Olyvia just laughed when she came in, "Pretty hungry, huh?" Yes I was, Darling, yes I was. I wasted no time and headed back on the road.

Once again, I was about to go through a major city at night. It's almost like I was acting out the Webster definition of insanity. With the ever so odd exception of Jacksonville, it is always a bad idea. This seemed to be truer in Florida because everyone here either drives 100 or is 100. As the sun set, the roads were illuminated with neon lights and paint jobs from sports cars, their engines sounding like they were tearing through space, and their racing exhausts ripping through Miami beach like they were filming a new Fast & Furious movie. Olyvia had called after leaving the restaurant with a car full of food for that night, nervous as all hell. Boston is a shitty place to drive, but I'll take that over Miami any day. White knuckling the wheel of her Altima rental, she told me she saw "at least 7 or 8, at least" crashes, in her own words.

Miami Beach is a place of vanity, with flashy cars and fake aesthetics everywhere. Wherever I looked, there were plastic people and their toys. As I gazed at buildings that touched the stars, I had the sudden urge to go to the bathroom and fast. (Funny what actually eating fiber will do to you.) This was the first time I had to use my bike lock the entire trip too. Not only was the place so sketchy and insanely busy, but this would have also been a ridiculous time to get my bike and all my stuff stolen, less than 200 miles from the finish.

The destination for the night was Florida City, the very last town in Florida before you get down to the Keys. I was about forty miles away, and my hopes for another pre-midnight finish were strong. I just had to conquer the late-night streets of Miami. There was no way that I wasn't going to be fighting to get through it. Another rule of the 10k is that each day has a new problem to solve. I was constantly waiting and paying attention for when one would rear its ugly head. All day had been pretty solid, but right as night began settling on the neon city, it became pretty clear I was in for five full rounds of an epic battle.

A storm had begun to roll in, lifting the palm trees up like plastic bags in a summer gust. As I was weaving though back streets and dodging cars taking blind corners, my dad called me to tell me that my tracker had stopped. With the exception of a couple hiccups, tracking for this had been really solid so far, and I was trying my best to keep it as accurate as possible. Underneath a tree in a Miami suburb, dodging a cliché Florida shower, I angrily mashed the buttons to restart it over and over, removed the batteries, spun them around, and anything else I could think of. The whole thing felt like I was pulling myself up a ladder of Laffy-Taffy. Pulling and climbing, virtually going nowhere. After twenty minutes I had to get moving again, which, ironically, helped to reconnect it to the satellites.

Despite the back roads, my route through Miami was going to be fairly straightforward. After a couple miles of some sketchy shit, I'd get onto a decent bike path used by the ACA. Leading into Miami was a gorgeous bridge, an asphalt red carpet laid out displayed the city lights like cameras at the Oscars. As I rolled over the water into the city, there were party barges and neon everywhere. You could almost smell the vodka and taste the cocaine in the air.

The entry was a gauntlet of oppressed members of society lashing out at me. The large homeless population shouted at me and kicked random bits of trash as I passed by, lights flashing. Since I was a neon beacon, I figured I'd blend in here, Miami camo. Unfortunately, my version of Miami chic with my five taillights made me look more like the fuzz than Tony Montana's smelly friend. I struggled to find the bike path. Directions were extremely unclear and there were absolutely no signs for it. I more stumbled upon it than intentionally found it. Nevertheless, I was elated to get away from everyone shouting at me. The second I found it though, it wasn't much better. If there were a place to get robbed and stabbed in Miami, it would be this path. The cracked and jagged roadway was pitch black and windier than a mountain pass. Since there were no markings or lights, I kept coming up to random intersections slamming off the curb and being forced to grab my brakes. It was evil, brutal torture on my tenderized hands. They were so swollen that everything hurt them; a constant dull ache radiated from my digits. With everything slowing me down, I was averaging 10 mph and constantly getting lost. Even in the daytime, this would have been harder than a five-year-old trying to find Waldo. You'd be coasting and all of a sudden end up in a bus terminal only to have to turn around. Nothing about its flow made any sense. With Route 1 visible just to my left, it was hard not to be jealous of the cars cruising by, but I wasn't that desperate yet. The Lamborghinis were still out in force blaring reggaeton and doing burn outs. Speed would really help me out, but not dying would help even more.

Even being so close, I had to take a break. I felt like I was moving at a constant pace but would never get there. The circumstances weren't catastrophic, but it felt like I was batting on a pinata filled with bees. A few won't hurt you, but if they all add up, they will kill you. My bike math being ever accurate, I was late and called Olyvia to let her know I'd be taking way longer than expected. Old habits die hard, so since I was stopped, I had to follow my water rule. On a mission, I grabbed another Smartwater from the 7-Eleven. The only other person in the store was some coked out day-trader yelling on his phone yelling about making huge multimillion deals. I can't imagine being so blind to the rat race that I needed validation from people around me to know I was rich. Buying my expensive water, I griped to the employees that I hated their stupid fucking bike path. Their reaction was some strange bag of emotion, equal parts fear and apathy. It was kind of ironic, the whole sight. A kind, small, middle-aged woman asked me if there was anything she could do? I thanked her, but only I could solve my problems.

The sooner that you realize you are the only one who can fix your problems, the sooner you find your power. We have an increasing dependence on other people to solve all our issues. It's almost like we can't sit with our emotions and work through something anymore. Coming head on to a problem and coming out the other side will make you stronger and more capable to take on the next mountain.

The time for this charade was done. I gave up on the "security" of the godforsaken bike path and jumped back on Route 1 with all the other idiots. Pulling onto the road, I turned on Stick Figure and tucked into my aero bars. It felt like being transported to a whole other dimension, some real-life Tron bike action. Eating up pavement at over 17 mph I was a fucking rocket ship going to a faraway galaxy. Since I was getting to the end of the line on this epic road, traffic was starting to thin out.

Even though there were signs everywhere saying "SHARE THE ROAD", people still honked and practically grazed me. Admittedly, there were far fewer assholes than I had expected. Before I had even realized it, I was pulling up to the motel where I'd finally have a companion.

Olyvia was there watching Jurassic Park. Just like Happy Gilmore, this was the second time where a movie I had daydreams about played on cable TV. I took this as another sign of my destiny. Eating soba noodles, chugging kombucha and coconut water, all gifts after working through such specific challenges today, everything felt like it was coming together just like it was meant to.

FLORIDA CITY, FL TO KEY WEST, FL

I WANTED TO START the final day like the first. No extra sleep was needed for the last day. The alarm was set for 5 a.m. so I could be out before the sun again. Unlike the first morning, the bottom of the US wouldn't be quite so frosty. I microwaved a cup of oatmeal, dumped all my extra gear and headed out the door. Olyvia took a picture of me just as I was leaving, and I could hardly recognize the man in the photo. His face was gaunt, worn, with a gruff and wiry beard, and his eyes were swollen, being dragged down by massive purple bags. He looked tired and tested but strong and durable, ready for the fight.

The air was thick and stagnant, not like a stuffy office though. More like the kind that evokes curiosity and wonder of what's to come before the heat of the day gets turned up to eleven. Fighting back tears, I started a Facebook Live video for the final day. The Everglades surrounded me like a single sheet on your bed in the middle of summer. Choking up between words, the reality of the scenario set in.

A vivid memory played through my head like a film projector. It was the middle of summer, and I was just getting back into training after the accident. I had to wake up extra early one Sunday to get in miles before attending to my "normal human" plans later. Riding through central-Massachusetts' rural farm towns before 7 a.m. on a Sunday, I found myself and one Harley-riding biker on an empty road. He passed me, with Bob Seger's Turn the Page on full blast. The saxophone hung in the still air as Bob sang about the life of the road. How its long hardships can make you feel so free and so lonely at the same time. This was my experience, and I was so fortunate to have it.

We have a tendency to let ourselves be distracted or tricked into thinking that our existence is limited to small, specific goals. For me, my depression and anxiety have always pulled me to the back of my mind, keeping me from the experience of living life. For others, it's working the 9 to 5 grind, but even this is a constant chase of something that exists only in our minds. When you are on vacation and come back people say, "Welcome back to reality!" The funny thing is that every experience is reality. The choices you make every day, consciously or subconsciously, make up your reality. Whether it's a social anxiety or a projected scenario, it's so easy to live in the back seat, letting the words of your peers be your GPS guiding you through life. Make the brash decision and take the leap; chase the adventure no matter the medium.

As it goes, just in the peak of my trip down nostalgia drive I got my first flat of the entire trip. I thought this was pretty amazing given that I had already covered 2150 miles in eleven days. Those Continental 4-Seasons were some serious, no-bullshit pieces of engineering. Though it broke me from my moment of gratitude, I was worried about my weak-ass hands. I couldn't even open a sealed water bottle, let alone bend rubber back over a piece of unforgiving metal. "Struggling" would be an apt descriptor for how people driving by would have described my open-road repair. Fumbling to first flip over the loaded bike, then to take out the skewer, were serious bouts of strength. In the process of putting a new tube in, I found a piece of glass the size of a .22 shell in my tire. This weapon of mass tire destruction had to be pulled out. In the process, I lost the spring for my rear quick release, a tiny, silver piece smaller than a marble that practically ran away from me. The fears I had been holding at bay started to come crashing down on me like a wave. But the reality of my goal bounced me back; I reminded myself that this wasn't over until I got to that damn buoy in Key West. I laid down on the pavement, searching for the spring like the murder weapon of a homicide. Finding it, I put everything back together. The whole ordeal took about a half hour. Oh man, was I grateful to have woken up early now.

Back on the road I could feel the bounce of my rear tire and knew I needed a stand-up bike pump to actually get me back to where I like it. I had researched shops before I'd started off because of the touristy nature of the area. Most "bike shops" here are just places where people rent beach cruisers with their families. Fortunately, a legit bike shop, All Keys Cycles, would be opening in Key Largo the exact time I could reach it. There were just ten miles between us.

Before I made it to Key Largo, I had my last interview with John, Joe, and Courtney over at WPOR. Their first call was timed with me riding over the bridge to the first island. It was hilariously windy on the phone. They called back just a couple minutes later, and it felt so familiar and nostalgic. Laughing like old friends, they wished me luck and asked a few closing questions. I can still hear Courtney saying, "You should write a book." I hope this makes you proud, guys.

All Keys Cycles was exactly what you would expect, a bike

shop with a surfer atmosphere. Everyone in there was so laid back it felt like there should have been hammocks everywhere. The owner was stoked about the journey, which really meant a lot. People often expressed amazement when they heard what I was doing out on the road. Truly though, few knew what it was like to actually live on the road doing big miles every day. He insisted to give me this drink mix which I really didn't want. It was one of those scenarios though where it's rude to not accept a gift, so I obliged my rad new friend. After a new tube and some fresh air, I was back on the A1A, the only road to the Keys.

The road was some great tarmac with only a few spots where I had to move over to avoid trash cans, mailboxes, and general debris. Luckily for me, this appeared to be a big cycling community. Somewhere that people seemed to expect a dude in spandex flying down the road on his six-inch saddle. The sun rose quickly and it was starting to get hot. Florida hot, like a humid bathroom with poor fucking ventilation and your wife showering in it.

I was drinking *constantly*. When cycling you should drink 12-16 oz of liquid per hour. In this weather I made sure to double it. My bottles went first, then the hydration bladder. Over and over in that order. Guzzling coconut water after coconut water, I retained absolutely everything, except the food I was eating.

At my first stop, waiting for me at the post office like a golden angel, Olyvia was in the car blasting the air conditioner with half a noodle bowl, fresh pressed juice, and more Smartwater. The juice was like drinking from the Holy Grail and its sweet nectar pulsed through my veins like an IV. It was absolutely nuclear. These nutrients had been all but absent in my diet for weeks now and I felt every inch of my body tingle. On top of my juice high, the veggie noodles made my heart skip a beat. Their crunchy texture combined with the cashew sauce was a fatty, carbohydrate delight that made me feel like a gladiator ready for war.

Soon after getting back on the road, I had the need to make an urgent bathroom stop. Fiber. It was kind of sad slyly slipping into one of my last roadside bathroom stops. The walls felt like they had no insulation and they certainly didn't absorb any sound. Wet wallpaper dripped down to the concrete floor creating small puddles, saturated even further by my pouring sweat. The attendant scowled at me for one of the last times, and I smiled at one of my final temporary companions on the way out.

Back on the road with reapplied sunscreen and a fully belly, I was soaring. The wind was at my back. There were also these magnificent cumulus clouds that covered me from the sun like cotton candy umbrellas. Though I could've actually ridden passed their shadows, I made sure to coast a little to enjoy them while I could. Other than my boy Oscar, these clouds were my first riding buddies since Rod in D.C. I couldn't believe the time I was making. Glancing at my Garmin I kept seeing 17-18 mph and I was hardly pushing the pedals. I started doing bike math, and, for once, it was in my favor. It was time to empty the tank and go for it. Time to hold nothing back and leave everything I had out there.

I was dancing on my nearly melting, 28mm razor blades. Slicing from left to right over the white line, narrowly missing the mile-long tails of iguanas as they scurried from my path. I was back on Mario Kart Rainbow Road all over again, dodging coconuts beside the tails of these tropical creatures. Next to me was only ocean, stretching wide to each horizon. At the water's edge, I saw swaths of floral board shorts under large umbrellas as people fished, their massive poles like boom mics on a TV set, stretching to capture anything in their path.

I changed islands quickly and often. The bridges between these little pond skips were like links in a chain. I kept hearing from people about a "seven-mile bridge", but all these bridges were huge in comparison to my tiny dot. I couldn't wait to see what this legendary behemoth looked like!

As the pavement changed from smooth to broken, I knew I had entered a different micro-ecosystem. That it smelled like sewage was also a dead giveaway I had made it to Big Pine Key. I was surrounded on all sides by a swamp home to the Key deer. In this protected habitat live these deer that are the size of dogs. Normally on these adventures I get to see all these far-out creatures. I was not so lucky this time, but, oh man, look up how adorable those fuzzy little guys are.

After meeting Olyvia at another roadside stop, finishing my noodles and juice, and reapplying some of my SPF 100 house primer, I was cooled and feeling like a rocket. A quick selfie and my last re-up on nutrition, I kissed Olyvia goodbye and sent her to Key West. She needed a break, and she deserved a few minutes to herself. My rock was finally able to settle into the earth while I sped down this two-lane highway.

Just like all other beautiful and unique parts of this country have been overtaken by big business and American consumerism, Marathon Key was no different. Out of thin air, your typical American strip mall materialized. Businesses and fast-food establishments covered both sides of the street just as if I had been in New England. The one upside was that I had infinite bathroom options. McDonalds, of all places, was my choice. Honestly though, that bathroom was fucking spotless!

Cooling my engine was just what the doctor ordered before the next part of the adventure, the Seven Mile Bridge.

I came upon the bridge in a bliss-filled flurry. Like a boxer at a speed bag, my focus heightened. I felt no pain and I blasted my attack upon the Goliath. As I scanned the scattered pieces of glass along the flying road's edges, apprehension set in. I would almost certainly be fucked if something happened right now. Just as that thought passed my mind, a huge gust blew off the ocean and hit my side. With white knuckles I gripped the bars and ripped my steed back under me. There was no way I was going down here. My only options were to keep control, be run over by a fleet of cars, or be sent tumbling sixty-five feet into the ocean below. Despite my determination, I did try to search for a ladder I could climb, bike in hand, to the finish.

When I rode cross country, I had read an excerpt of a book called "Godspeed" about bicycle travel. The book was all about one man, Robert Linz, and what he learned cycling around the US after the recession. The premise was that your thoughts put you into the scenario of fear that you're imagining. You project yourself into whatever fear you are dreaming, or nightmare-ing up. The logic though, applies to all aspect of life. Ever wonder how two people, living the exact same experience can have two completely different perspectives? I must have been only twelve when a neighborhood girl invited me to a haunted house. This was honestly my worst nightmare. She lived at the front of a campground, a literal horror movie. My extreme imagination already kept me awake every night as I felt too vulnerable to fall asleep. When we entered the first cabin, my friend clung to my arms in pure freight. Being the manly sixth grader, I had to look brave for Julia. Putting up a front, I appeared calm (so I thought...), and everything became less terrifying for an instant. When people jumped out of corners with chainsaws, I tried laughing in their faces. Even though I was actually scared shitless, my mood changed. We went through the entire thing and I felt like a war hero. Think of how some people run 100-mile footraces through the night in the middle of the woods and how the settlers thought demons lived on the woods edge. We only experience the emotional field we put ourselves in, fake chainsaws or not.

When I turned my fear off, I noticed the nearly infinite species of birds around me. Pelicans and white herons perched elegantly upon long beautiful legs speckled the coast. Like fighter pilots, V-shaped wings dive bombed towards the water in an effort to find food. My grip loosened and, just like that, I was flowing again. Mashing the pedals like an easy Sunday ride, I broke 20 mph and blasted through the belly of that beast. I bombed down the backside of the Seven Mile Bridge and sped off to the next island on my path.

With my speed I was covering more ground that I thought. Mary from D.C. reached out to ask for my arrival time, and as I chewed up time, I kept having to update her as I rode to tell her earlier and earlier. With the finish line nearly close enough to grab, I was shooting for time. I kept telling myself, "Stay focused," anytime a thought would creep in. There were only twenty-five miles between me and the fabled end.

Anyone who has ever experienced a flow state knows it's hard to describe. Something like the interconnection between everything that you are, encapsulated in this one moment. I had been listening to the same two Stick Figure albums on repeat all day. The dub had me floating and kept my focus when I received phone call after phone call of friends wanting to congratulate me. To me, they were trying to pull me out, and I just couldn't let it happen; I had to ignore them all. Blowing past a few bikers, tucked into my aero bars, I laughed at what they probably thought of me, not knowing that I had just traveled 2300 miles in eleven days. My heart was bursting with love. I kept watching my phone and Garmin *click, click, click* as the miles ticked away one by one.

15 … 14 … 13 …

There was no way anything was going to stop me.

5··· 4··· 3···

I hit the final red light, vibrating with energy as the finish loomed. Since Key West is an actual city, of course I still had to get lost one last time. Tunnel vision was at an all-time high. Chickens now darted across the street, and I laughed at what a funny ending it would be if I crashed now. Every house was a different color that blended together at the edges of my vision. I weaved out of the path of rented scooters and ripped tight turns to the last stretch.

The centripetal force of destiny pulled me to the buoy over the cobblestone's corner. I saw Olyvia's face, glowing with relief as I left a trail of fire and made my silent attack upon the marker. Like a dog ready to attack, I was low and sprinting. I grabbed my breaks and skidded to a stop and checked my Garmin. Her Facebook Live stream rolling, she cheered, and I paused for what seemed like forever. "You have to touch it!" she screamed. I unhooked myself from John Quick. His release was like a mother bird and her nest, telling me to fly. I skipped the massive line, stomped over and made a thunderous slap against the world-famous buoy.

"90 Miles to Cuba"

2280 miles: 11 days, 9 hours, 32 minutes.

I had a couple interviews in the moments after the finish. An NPR reporter was there, and I had a phone call with US1 radio shortly after. The whole thing was a blur. I dropped off my bike with Island Bicycles, the best shop on Key West. It was a ceremonious experience handing over John Quick and all my bags. The road had taken hold of us and the scraps of our story were disgusting to be honest. After days in the rain and never fully cleaning my food bags, they had rotting granola bars in them. The rank smell nearly made me yack all over their concrete floor. I took a picture with the owner and mechanic and then shook hands with the caretakers of John Quick. Thankfully, they gave me a cotton shirt to replace my jersey.

After handing over my best buddy, Olyvia and I grabbed a sit-down meal. There was still an overwhelming feeling of *GO*. I took a hobo shower in the sink of this vegan island cafe and we tried to take it all in. My first beer fizzed through my bloodstream, and I clinked glasses with my wife as I gazed into her beautiful brown eyes. Ultra-cycling is a lonely endeavor, and this ending was just the two of us, something I would never change.

AFTERWORD

I FLEW HOME THE following day in a complete haze, arriving back in Boston at 1 a.m. Our best friends Mike and Nicole were there at Logan waiting to bring us home. My hands were absolutely wrecked, and my hair was nearly one giant dread-lock. The months following the 10k involved a lot of rehab on my hands to get strength and dexterity back. After completing some grip strength testing, my hands resembled the strength of an eighty-year-old woman. I couldn't ride outside at all; no pressure could be put on my ulnar nerves. The dull pain turned into a constant ache, heavily affected by temperature. The transition back to normal life was made all the more difficult since I didn't have my bike as an outlet. Because I could only really use my thumbs, the first draft of this book was written entirely on my iPhone.

It took months to submit all my evidence to Guinness. I was solo and unsupported for most of the ride, so everything relied on my GPS data and memory. I had to call dozens of businesses and describe who I was and the verification I needed. Everyone remembered me immediately—I was not their typical customer. On May 7th, 2020, a year to the day of that fateful car collision, I became the official Guinness World Record Holder for *The Fastest Crossing of the United States by Bicycle North to South.*

Despite all of the hard work, we didn't reach our goal of $10,000 for NAMI after the ride. While we pulled in an amazing $6,500, the entire objective was to reach the 10k mark. I came up with a fresh adventure then started down the long road of learning a new ultra-discipline. On September 19th, 2020, I set off to run 100 miles in under 24 hours across the entire length of Cape Cod. After completing the journey, the run was picked up by a news broadcast in Boston and I finally reached my goal. Finally hitting my fundraising goal was one of my most proud and fulfilled moments in my entire life.

I hope that this book helps you find something in yourself, whatever that may be. Remember that you always have more that you think. Even when everything is lost, you are broken and feel lifeless, there is hope. Keep working to be better every day. Keep pushing even when the times get tough; that is what will make you achieve more than you ever could imagine.

THANK YOU!!!

THE COMMON CLICHÉ is that "it takes a village", and this was no exception.

First and foremost, thank you to my loving and supporting wife, Olyvia. Without you, I'd be nothing. For all the sleepless nights you are by my side. Thank you for understanding this dream and being there for me every step of the way. You knew that this was bigger than me and what I was trying to accomplish with this. You are the love of my life, my best friend and soul mate. I can't thank you enough.

Mike Robinson: Without you, this probably never would've happened. Not only did you do all the photo, video, audio AND editing for this project, you were always there. When the project first fell apart, and again and again… You called me every day on the road and are there when I need you most. Playing Eye of the Tiger, telling me who I am, and saddling up in the freezing rain. You are my brother.

Matt Perez: The third piece of the 10k Crew to form the

pyramid. Always thinking about the big picture and the philosophy of life. If there is anyone who gets this part of my life, it's you, and I can't thank you enough. You and the Crew saved me with "the conference call" and helped whip everything together after it all crumbled that day leaving CT. You give me perspective and strength to forge though when the lights are off and everyone is asleep.

Dan & Ian: My oldest friends and the mapping HQ. I will never forget the night around the fire at the house I grew up in when I told you I was going to ride cross country. You are my brothers and our memories will live on forever. ·

Max: You have always had an ability to make me laugh when I don't want to. Someone who has literally fought for me, more than once. I know you always have my back, and I'll always have yours.

Tim: Thank you for having the weirdest sleep schedule that always aligns with my adventures. It's beyond serendipitous. Thanks for picking up my calls in the dead of the night and making me laugh. Love to you, the boys, and Pha.

My Parents: I know that these adventures keep you up at night. Thank you for supporting me even though it probably weighs heavier on you than me. I truly can't thank you both for all you have done for me my entire life.

Sarah: The one who I count roadkill with. You are the reason I started running everyday back in middle school. You showed me hiking and so much. Thanks for always picking up the phone and laughing with me at my ridiculous misfortune. It's still Monday.

Maine Bike Works: You guys helped me out when no one else would. The support you gave me made me feel like a rockstar even when doors were constantly slammed in my face. MBW lives for adventure.

Tamara: You helped me before and after the 10k. My knees, ankles, and then hands thank you so much for all of your help. You really care about the patients you see, and the world thanks you.

Hank "The Wizard": My guru and my healer. Thank you for taking time with me on early mornings just when the gym opened. You helped me prepare to the 10k and wind down afterwards. Your help spanned physically, mentally, and spiritually. Thank you for your healing.

Jimmi: The man behind the carbon. Thank you so much for all the help and guidance with my bike getting ready for this. You saw something in me that many other shops didn't. Your help at Harris Cyclery was invaluable. You are an amazing mechanic and musician. Thanks for building up John Quick to the beast that he is!

Ralf: Thanks for always supporting me and my adventures. I'm so happy we crossed paths that day in Medora! You're a great person and friend, we still have to ride Europe!

Mary: Thank you so much for letting a stinky stranger stay at your house on the whim of a phone call. You have such a kind soul and care so deeply. Everything you did from letting me stay, cooking me food, and lining up press in Key West made this adventure what it was. I am so grateful for everything you did to help!

Rod: What a great ride we had together, brother! You have an ability to block out nonsense that most people shudder at. You helped me through the night and woke up at the crack of dawn to ride on a ridiculous highway with me. Thanks for sharing the road with me!

Georgia Mike: Your help with picking up my food and hanging out not only fueled my nutritionally depleted body but also my soul. Speaking with you for that time really brought me back. You and Connie are special people with exceptionally large hearts. Thanks for my best break of the whole adventure.

Lynn Salvo: Thanks for introducing me to some amazing human beings and all your support. You're inspiration for me to ride far for years to come.

I am a very fortunate human being to have so many great people in my life. Please don't think I don't love you if I missed you.

Jamie, Steve, Meagan, Jake, Scott McCoy, Nicole, The Moulton's, The O'Connels, Hanna, Nichole, Jerry, Scotty & Marissa, Crocco, The Molloys, Nick & Em, Connor & Shay, Harris Cyclery, Billy from SC, Spencer at GWR, John, everyone who works with me at Lesley (especially my TSS crew), Doug, Amy, Matt Landry, Steve from WS in VT, Jon Joe & Courtney at WPOR, and so many others.

Be Good To Each other!

Love,

B

Gear List

Bike Details

- Bike: GT Grade Carbon 53cm
- Drivetrain:Shimano Ultegra
- Gearing: 50/34 11-32
- Brakes: TRP Spyre Mechanical
- Saddle: ISM PN 3.1
- Bars: Whiskey Parts Co No.07 12F Alloy, Profile Design Clip-on Aero bars
- Wheels: Dt Swiss R470 32/36
- Hubs: Schmidt Son 28 (front), Hope Pro 4 (rear)
- Tires: Continental Grand Prix 4-season
- Front Lighting: Sinewaves Beacon, NiteRider Lumina 900
- Rear Lighting: NiteRider Solas 250, Serfas Thunderbolt- 3

Electronics

- Garmin Fenix 5x Watch
- Garmin 520
- SPOT GEN3
- iPhone 7

- Rav Power 10,000mAh power bank
- Anker 4 Port Brick

Clothing

- GoreTex Rain Jacket
- GoreTex Rain Pants
- Pearl Izumi hi-viz Shoe Covers
- Sugoi RC Pro Chamois (2)
- Giro Cycling Gloves
- Sugoi Knee Warmers
- Smartwool Socks
- Darn Tough Cycling Socks

Sleep System

- Black Diamond Twilight Bivy
- LL Bean Down Jacket
- Klymit X-lite 3/4 Sleeping Pad

Bags

- Revelate Designs Mountain Feed Bags (2)
- Revelate Designs Gas Tank
- Revelate Designs Tangle Frame Bag (small)
- Revelate Designs Terrapin 8L Seat Pack

- Camelback 2L Hydration pack

Tools

- Pedros Mini Tool
- Park Tool Patch Kit
- Spare Tube (3)
- Zip Ties Taped To Rear Triangle
- Tyre Levers (4)
- Spare Brake/Shift Cables
- Spare Brake Pads
- Patch Repair Kit-Half Self-Stick, Half Glue
- Extra AAA Batteries For SPOT

WHERE WILL YOUR NEXT ADVENTURE BE?

NOTES